My friends
Bill - to a treasured
past, an ancient
book, and a delicious
tomorrow —
love
Leo Tolstoy-

Conrad

a
sack
full
of sun

"Them folk you been runnin' by me, they pretty good folk you know. Put 'em in your hat and you ain't gonna get rained on. I mean . . . put 'em in a bag, brother, and you got a sack full of sun."

a sack full of sun

by
Conrad Balfour

Dillon Press
MINNEAPOLIS

Library of Congress Cataloging in Publication Data

Balfour, Conrad, 1928-
  A sack full of sun.

  Autobiographical.
  1. Balfour, Conrad, 1928-   I. Title.
E185.97.B2A36   977.6'05'0924 [B]   74-8763
ISBN 0-87518-074-4

to Joe Archie, Brother

If I looked hard I could see his face. Had he wanted to, he might have shaved. The bristles are black and gray and they stick one by one into the brown of his skin. The head is bowed and he sits with elbows and arms on thighs. The hands are clenched one into the other. I whisper his name: "Joe." He does not move. His eyes are closed and he does not move.

preface

"I don't know. So much of what you say hits me hard. It was so much of you. Still . . . there's a quality that doesn't seem to capture the loving person I know you to be. Maybe it's some of the curses. Maybe that's where you were then. But now. I think you're in a different place. And I think you should tell people that."

Mary is the person I love the most. We were discussing the original manuscript for this book. And Mary was right. I have changed. There are some places I can look back to and recognize that I was wrong. There may be other places where I was wrong and I still haven't recognized them. This book does not pretend to be right at the expense of those who saw it another way. But I do know that as Commissioner of Human Rights my life changed, and since those stormy days my life has changed again. Age, experience, do I dare say wisdom?

Out of it all, I have come to cherish two beliefs: first, that the greatest risk in our society is to tell the truth; and second, that we must learn to exclaim to a stranger the words "I love you." For love, undenied, unquestioned, is the only way this planet of ours will be salvaged.

To write this book I needed encouragement and criticism. That came first from Pat and Dick Fontaine, and then from Uva Dillon. A firstborn needs tender care and love, thus my thanks to editor Helen Tegenfeldt. I would also like to acknowledge the assistance of Sim Heller, Wayne Konga, Gordon Locksley, George Shea, Elva Walker, Bob McGarvey, and Harry Davis, who provided the funds for me to become involved with the Pitts-Lee case in Florida.

a sack full of sun

one

Chiseled and chipped,

bearing brunt of wind and slap of rain,

some with intolerable lean, others

with snappish erect,

set in the sod for some who would pause . . .

these are a few of my wayside markers.

Gonna get me my fix

and stay out of jail

Gonna get me my fix

at the altar rail

W hen I was very small, I learned about Confession and Communion and Three Gods in One. I'd go to church on Sunday in different areas of Boston's South End. The Immaculate Conception, which had my favorite color blue on most of the walls. The Cathedral of the Holy Cross with its hidden rooms. The French Church, so quiet on weekdays. The Franciscan Church with its priests who wore sandals.

I had just had a rehearsal, the week before, on how to properly receive Communion. For some reason, on this Sunday, I attended the German Church. It was an interesting landmark in Boston, with a steeple that had been partly blown off during a summer hurricane. When Communion was celebrated, I knelt in young anticipation for reception of the Christ Body. As the Host touched my mouth, I experienced a taste of revulsion. The bland bread was totally rejected by my taste buds, and as a result I marched back to the pews, hands clasped, with the holy matter suspended between the roof of my mouth and my tongue. When Mass ended I ran outdoors and spit the soft, wet, separated, unleavened bread into the street. It splattered on the pavement in a mixture of white saliva and dough, and to me it looked like pigeon droppings. I knew then I was going to die, and when I died I'd go to hell. No sense in confessing to a priest. Neither he nor anyone else could save me now. I had just spit out God into the same streets that were baptized daily with horse manure, dog turds, and human urine.

Years later, in my late teens, I finally confessed that secret shame to an Irish priest. He told me that I had blasphemed God's Body. He told me that what I had done was a grave misfortune. I carried that shame for many years of my life.

That wasn't enough. There were other shames. The neighborhood I grew up in was crawling with con men, hoods, and gangsters. My Uncle Edmund was one of them. I loved him, but I was never proud of his Mafia ties. I was ashamed of the clothes I wore, mostly knickers with a hole and a flap for a fly. I was ashamed of not knowing who my mother and father were — and more afraid that if I found out I'd be ashamed of them, too. I was ashamed of "hooking" high school my complete senior year and still graduating because I was captain of the track team . . . of touching Viola on a "sinful" part of her anatomy . . . and I was ashamed to be black. My family wanted me to "pass," since I was as light as any Italian or Syrian in the city. For thirty years I carried this guilt.

Then one day a man named Stan King practically ordered me to work with him on a poverty program. For the next five years, including those as Minnesota's Commissioner of Human Rights, I erupted in explosive confrontation with anything opposed to human dignity. I sometimes lost sight of prudence and tact and common sense. I reacted with my heart and often frightened well-meaning peers with my outbursts. But those turbulent years helped to cleanse me.

I found that there is no bible on earth strong enough to convince me that Jews are inferior. No historic literature to show that Christians are superior to *anybody*. To live as Christ is a marvelous undertaking, but to deny Indians their Great Spirit is to commit armed religious robbery. Neither Christ, Buddha, nor Muhammad has a corner on "good."

I found that not only religious bodies, but governments, too, commit crimes. One day the black inmates of Sandstone Prison put on a play about violence and jails and policy numbers and dope. In one scene, a powerful gangster is being grilled by federal agents.

Fed: Do you have any knowledge of the young children in Center City taking narcotics?

Gangster: No sir.

Fed: Do you know of the high stake gambling in this city?

Gangster: No sir.

Fed: Are you aware of the three killings this last week?

Gangster: No sir.

Fed: Have you anything to do with prostitution on Third Avenue?

Gangster: No sir. You must be mistaking me for the United States Government.

The playwright knew, as I now knew, that guilt lay heavy in places other than Sandstone . . . that governments are made up of people, and governments commit major crimes. And religious bodies commit major crimes. Majorities and minorities, writers and readers, the titled and the nameless . . . all commit crimes. Though we are of like flesh, it is only the few doing their penance for all of the unwounded others.

Buck, Buck,

How many fingers have I got up?

One, two, three, or none?

Fingers up you have but one.

Wrong. Wrong you son of a gun.

Load on your back has just begun.

1970

In January, the governor asked me to take the job of Commissioner of Human Rights for the state of Minnesota. I accepted. In a few days I would be officially appointed to that office. The week preceding my move to the new position had a certain set to it — everyday incidents were easier to recall, more memorable, a point of departure from the "old" life and a bridge to the "new." The days trotted across the calendar's path something like this:

Sunday

On came the Sunday mystique. I arose from bed as if it were a Sunday. The world looked like a Sunday. Even the morning felt like a Sunday morning. I had plenty of time to shave, dress, and down a Sunday kind of breakfast before driving to Mass.

The Basilica was only a short drive from my apartment

and today I would be a lector. The cathedral had been adding innovative touches to its services for three years now. Each Sunday, at each Mass, teams of lectors and commentators were petitioned to serve in this great church named for the Virgin Mother Mary.

Outside, it was bright and colder than before. Winter had long given notice to Fall that its lease was at an end. The Basilica is built on a slight rise and can easily be seen from many parts of Minneapolis, the high dome resting atop the imposing edifice. Below, as silent subjects, are smaller buildings — school, chapel, rectory.

Inside the cathedral, eight confessionals stand crypt-like, formidable, and cold. Each has framed walnut doors. Each is punctured with white tacks holding white cards announcing white priests. On either side is an entrance for sinners. The vast ceiling arches in slow ascension to a height of 187 feet. From its center, black rods stretch outward, with tentacles of short rods rayed out spiderlike from their lower ends. Each ray has a black hoodlamp, and from within, unseen bulbs struggle to send light downward. Each lamp is a cowled monk . . . hidden, hooded, hunched.

I skipped up the street steps, down an aisle, and into the sacristy. Father Coleman was dressing with great ceremony. Something was said in Latin. The commentator was already at the altar. Two boys dipped fingers into holy water and touched them to mine and Father's in a creation scene. We crossed ourselves and filed out to a waiting congregation.

Mass was celebrated swiftly. When Communion was offered, three additional priests came to assist. I saw there was need for more altar assistance. One duty was to handle a silver plate, which was held under the recipient's chin to catch the blessed Host if, on rare occasion, one slipped from the hold of the serving priest.

I decided to walk the rail.

Down I came from my private pew, selected a polished, mirrored silver plate, and fell in step beside the bishop. Our portion of the communion rail was at one end, the last few feet of it curving back to a high iron gate. People flocked quietly to the rail in rows of twelve. The bishop placed the Hosts gently on silent tongues. Some thrust their tongues fully forward. Others barely forward. Some shyly emerged, and after brief hesitation by the bishop's Hosted hand, they reluctantly offered more landing area.

The faces were of great interest. I never before imagined how ludicrous one looked with eyes closed and tongue protruding . . . how many shapes there would be . . . how much variety in shades and widths, even in velocity — from lethargic lowering and lifting to daredevilish dancing and darting. Children bent their heads back with no self-consciousness. Young men did it with sureness; old men with slowness; elderly ladies with facial screwing. Yet it was beautiful. Each head raised in anticipation of the living Body. Each pair of hands clasped in private prayer.

We glided to our right, the bishop ambling forward and sliding backward. One by one he took a single round Host from the chalice and shook it free of ghostly moisture before placing it lightly upon a waiting tongue. Occasionally he let his eyes drift to the row of people waiting patiently to replace those now kneeling.

"Body of Christ."

"Amen."

"Body of Christ."

"Amen."

Eyes were opened. As we approached they would close, and as we passed they would again open.

This man's face was gray and his hair was gray and the Host glowed on his gray tongue.

"Body of Christ."

This round face was blind. Like the others, she, too, closed her eyes and when we passed she opened them once again.

"Amen."

We were now two from the end. The bishop's hand dipped into the chalice, and thumb and forefinger emerged again with the diminutive sacrament. He placed it on the tongue of a man. Maybe a woman. I'm not sure. As his hand made the return motion, another Host flew off from his fingers and scaled kite-like between two kneelers and out of my sight. No one seemed to notice. The procession of priest and layman continued. The kneelers knelt. The receivers received. The people up forward gave way to those behind. The bishop took Host. Gave Host. Took Host. Gave.

"Oh my God!" I thought. "It must be crushed under someone's shoes!"

I wanted to tell him that he had lost a wafer. I almost did. The courage left me as we moved along. Why hadn't people seen it and tried to pick it up? Or drawn his attention to it? Why hadn't the bishop seen it? Surely he must have seen it! Why did no one speak out? Wasn't the Body of Christ sacred?

I remembered once attending church in Sanborn, North Dakota, where the priest dropped a Host on his return to the communion table. He quickly got a small linen cloth and covered the fallen matter until Mass was completed. Afterwards, he carefully picked up the bread and washed the floor with dedicated ceremony. Why hadn't our bishop stopped his ritual, sent me back for linen, and administered to the Body of Christ?

Mass soon ended and we said our farewells and thank-yous in the sacristy. I returned to the altar rail with foreboding. I knew my chances of seeing what I hoped to find were slight. The church was almost dark now, and many feet surely must have ground the bread into dust.

But down against the marble, there where it came to right angles with step and rail, was a flash of white . . . the Host . . . untouched, unsmirched, unbroken. Like the bishop, I picked it up in thumb and forefinger, placed it in the palm of my hand, and returned to the sacristy. Father Coleman was still ridding himself of his vestments.

"Look, Father."

"Where did you get that?" He said it solemnly and low.

"I found it at the altar rail."

"Thank you, Conrad."

He removed it from my palm and turned away. I left the church.

The sun was bright and warm and inescapable. Church-goers were ascending the twenty-seven stairs to the darkness within. Another Mass would soon begin. Another lector would recite an epistle, another commentator would lead the followers in a psalm. Another Communion would be celebrated.

"Body of Christ."

"Amen."

Monday

It was one of those mushrooms that sprout up in every suburb: a supermarket, a drugstore, retail shops, pizza and ice cream joints, a launderette, a barber shop. I needed a hair cut, so I headed for the barber shop. The revolving red and white pole told me where to point my feet, but not whether the barber would cut my hair. Of course I knew he would. I had on a brown business suit — conservative. My starched shirt was Arrow and you had to be in close to see the subdued brown stripes. The tie was college, the shoes slip-on but not flashy, the topcoat navy blue. I figured he might guess me Italian or something similar. Although my hair was different from the hair barbers usually cut, I knew they'd be expert if they thought me Caucasian. I could be slick-back and rooster's ass like Valentino and if they thought me black they'd pull the no-experience routine like: "They got a good barber down on Penn Avenue . . . do ya justice."

Well, he did cut my hair. Even made conversation, despite my try for reading the paper in silence. On the sports page he saw snaps of the Vikings' Eller and picked it up from there. In the entertainment section he commented on dirty movies and "whaddya think of this crummy world?" When I gasped at a double suicide he let me know that he had gasped too and "could ya believe it?"

A small lady walked in with two children and asked for her favorite barber. He was no longer with the shop. She then gave some specific instructions and laid everyone out laughing.

"I want their hair cut and I want it SHORT! Get it? And I want it cut GOOD! Get it? I DON'T want a crew cut, but I don't want to come back here in a WEEK to get it cut again! IF YOU . . . KNEW . . . HOW HARD . . . IT WAS . . . TO GET THEM . . . OVER HERE . . . YOU'D BE PAYING ME TEN PERCENT!"

"Fine, lady. Do you want the back high?"

"HIGH?! CUT . . . IT . . . OFF! OFF! IN THE BACK LEAVE HIM ONLY HIS HEAD! ROSS! BART! I'm leaving now. When I get back, I expect this building to still be standing right here."

She was a funny woman.

Wednesday

Drew Johnson was in charge of group dynamic training at a poverty program which recruited businesses that would hire the poor and the untrained. Jobs were scarce and definitely not a joking matter. This morning when I walked into the training room, Drew had them going through the ropes. He was assuming the role of a personnel interviewer, while trainees took turns answering his loaded questions. It was a good exercise and certainly much tougher than what they would in reality encounter.

An attractive black woman walked in and sat down next to Cool Charles, who had already completed his turn at role-playing. She was tall and large-breasted with a bright red Afro. They called her Big Bertha and enjoyed exchanging banter with her.

Bertha asked, "What are they doing?"

Cool Charles answered, "He's laying a job interview on us. We s'pose to learn how to act."

Bertha looked him straight in the face and with complete composure said, "Has he hired anyone yet?"

Friday

Slowdrive was chunky small. His hair was greased straight back but would not stay down. It kept flopping up whenever he moved forward or if he bobbed his head . . . a rooster's comb drawing comic attention.

"Hi, Slowdrive. This is my last day of work here. The

boss figured maybe I could rap with you. He thinks you don't have much to do. That your paycheck is too big."

Slowdrive raised his hands like a baseball umpire checking for rain.

"Mr. Conrad. You know me. I'm not a heathen. I'm a Christian. I've been on this here job for sixteen years. There been noooo problem. I does my work. I shines my shoes. I ask for mo' work when the shine go slow. A man like me maybe has problems . . . personal. That's natchral. But I does my work. I DOES MY WORK! Now that jus' makes me up and mad! All the man need do is TALK to me! Like a CHRISTIAN! You don't bother a busy man like you. They talk to ME! To ME! Isn't that right, Mr. Conrad? They talk to ME! I'm reasonable. I'm easy to get along with. Now ain't I now? AIN'T I? Shoot. I've had adjustin' to do. I admits it. Wife died in May. That takes a whooool lot out of a man. A whooool lot. Then I gets me the bads once or twice. Ya see? THAT takes adjustin'. A man don't get used to not havin' his woman around. I'm a man, Mr. Conrad. I'm a man, ya know what I'm sayin'? And I'll tell ya somethin' . . . a man has needs. You understand? I got this woman. She tries to tell me I need carin'. Weeeell, I divided her a couple of times. Sure was hard to raise . . . me bein' sick and all. But I dinked her. Dinked her good. And I'm gonna keep on dinkin' her. Gonna take real good care of my health. Thas first. Work hard. Care for my diet. And maybe get a dink in now and then. There ain't no one need to complain to you. Not about me! They talks to ME, Mr. Conrad! They talks to ME!"

STATE OF MINNESOTA EXECUTIVE DEPARTMENT
HAROLD LEVANDER, GOVERNOR OF MINNESOTA

TO CONRAD BALFOUR OF HENNEPIN COUNTY, SENDS GREETING:

REPOSING ESPECIAL TRUST AND CONFIDENCE IN YOUR PRUDENCE, INTEGRITY AND ABILITY, I HAVE APPOINTED YOU, THE SAID CONRAD BALFOUR AS COMMISSIONER OF THE DEPARTMENT OF HUMAN RIGHTS, FOR A TERM EFFECTIVE JANUARY 14, 1970, AND EXPIRING THE FIRST MONDAY IN JANUARY, 1971, PURSUANT TO MINNESOTA STATUTES 363.04. YOU ARE, THEREFORE, BY THESE PRESENTS, APPOINTED AND COMMISSIONED AS COMMISSIONER OF THE DEPARTMENT OF HUMAN RIGHTS AS AFORESAID, TO HAVE AND TO HOLD THE SAID OFFICE AS COMMISSIONER OF THE DEPARTMENT OF HUMAN RIGHTS TOGETHER WITH ALL THE RIGHTS, POWERS, AND EMOLUMENTS TO THE SAID OFFICE BELONGING, OR BY LAW IN ANYWISE APPERTAINING, UNTIL THIS COMMISSION SHALL BE BY ME, OR OTHER LAWFUL AUTHORITY, SUPERSEDED OR ANNULLED, OR EXPIRE BY FORCE OR REASON OF ANY LAW OF THIS STATE.

IN TESTIMONY WHEREOF, I HAVE HEREUNTO SET MY HAND AND CAUSED THE GREAT SEAL OF THE STATE OF MINNESOTA TO BE AFFIXED AT THE CAPITOL IN THE CITY OF SAINT PAUL, THIS TWELFTH DAY OF JANUARY IN THE YEAR OF OUR LORD, ONE THOUSAND NINE HUNDRED SEVENTY AND OF THE STATE THE ONE HUNDRED TWELFTH.

HAROLD LEVANDER

How many fingers have I got up?

One, two, three, or none?

Fingers up my guess is two.

Wrong. Wrong you dirty jew.

Hmmmm. Niggers, spics, and homos too.

Thom Higgins was young and on top of the world. Very simply, he had a job. But he was fired from his job. He was dismissed after revealing that he was gay. Between the Department of Human Rights and the Minneapolis Civil Liberties Union he was unable to acquire redress. Our department just didn't know what to do about it. At a high voltage staff meeting, we tossed out every avenue of approach possible. Did we have jurisdiction? What would a case like this do to our legislative requests at the next session? Did we have the duty and obligation to protect *all* peoples?

We had another meeting, this time with Higgins and his friend Jack Baker, a young law student. We were impressed by both these young men. Still, I was persuaded to back off, to leave the case alone. Later I was to regret this decision. As the months went along I realized that my timidity was based more on politics than on dignity. I was simply afraid. It was another lesson to learn. Never back off from people's rights. Never.

But something did come of it all. Our department organized a task force to look into Minnesota gay life and examine the inadequacy of laws that protect only heterosexuals. We announced publicly that the purpose of this task force was to identify the problems faced by the homosexual minority in the state and to educate the public concerning them.

The news media was kind. But that was all. Wherever I went I overheard nasty remarks. Letters came to the office. Phone calls from anonymous heroes took up my time. Some in the black community were highly critical. Why the hell wasn't I fighting for the rights of blacks and Indians? At public appearances I was called a fag. A year later the governor was to say that of all the commissioners he had appointed, I was the weakest, because I too often strayed into areas in which I and the department had no jurisdiction.

It was too late for protestations. The task force was formulated. From this point on, there was no turning back.

"Hi. Balfour speaking."

"Is this Commissioner Balfour?"

"Hi. Right."

"I'm speaking for a group of people, commissioner, who'd like your reaction to registering a complaint on behalf of Snuffy."

"Who's Snuffy?"

"It was in all the news! Robert T. Smith had a column."

"Oh yes. Well, you must realize that we can't do anything for you."

"I know it's not the usual request, commissioner. I don't want to take your time, but we do have a point. A snowmobile that intrudes upon nature discriminates against animals."

"The state statute on discrimination includes only those categories that refer to people."

"But by discriminating against animals, it . . . the snowmobile, that is . . . discriminates against those of us who love animals."

"That may very well be the case. However, I'm afraid there is nothing I can do."

"But, commissioner, in this case a young child lost her pet. A very low-type person ran over her dog Snuffy. This is certainly within the domain of a department that is named for human rights."

"No sir, it isn't."

"Goddamn it! You protect criminals and those homos!"

"Take it easy."

"Will you listen to us? Can we visit with you?"

"No sir."

"Fuck you!"

Oh Yahhhh Man
You can turn your head

Oh Yahhhh Man
You can turn your heart

Oh Yahhhh Man
You can turn
You can turn the truth

But Ain't No Turning Back
Ya Hear
No Turning Back

No No
No No
Ya Hear
Oh No
But Ain't No Turning Back

It was to be just another talk . . . some people from the northeast side of town, a community group, with the normal problems of finding a speaker from meeting to meeting. The program chairman had sent my office a letter. Jan got my okay and sent the affirmative reply. I didn't name a topic — I hardly ever did. It made it difficult for printed programs, but this meeting was informal anyway.

It was dark out, and finding my way in the Cities had always been a chore for me. The visor of my car held the neat information slip that Jan always made out for me: name of group, place, date, time, number of people, length of talk. Still, I was having trouble finding my street. Highway 65 had a thousand shops and any one of them could help direct me to my destination. For some reason I stopped my car before a barroom. I left the motor running and skipped through the cold into a tough-looking tavern. The man behind the counter was big and bald and anything but busy. I asked for directions and he went to great lengths to get me on a correct course.

A gruff voice halted me as I was about to sprint out to the warmth of my car, newly confident that I'd be on time for the meeting.

"Are you Commissioner Balfour?"

"Uh huh."

He pulled a pistol from within his corduroy shirt, pointed it straight at my stomach, and pulled the trigger. Nothing happened. No explosion. No flame. I'm not even sure if I heard anything, but it must have jammed. My mind in a crazy whim of timing flashed back to days of boyhood in Boston. Uncle Edmund was running a tailor shop as a front for the numbers rackets. One of his bettors walked up to the cash register and jerked a pistol up to his chest. The weapon jammed and the man fled. Edmund looked for him for months, vowing to kill him.

I turned around and walked out. My back tingled. Someone shouted. It could have been the big, bald man. The car was warm and the directions were precise. I remember them. My talk? I don't know. Never heard a word of it.

I was feeling low. Emily Ann Staples of the Women's Advisory Committee suggested that I visit the Minneapolis Institute of Art. They were exhibiting the great photo collection of Richard Avedon. One wing of the building was given over to his works. Much had been written in the papers about his genius, and I knew it would be exciting, but I hadn't generated enough enthusiasm to take it in. Emily Ann was usually on target with her suggestions, though, so I decided to follow her advice.

Anne Whiton, a dear friend, happily accompanied me to the collection. Neither one of us, as well as thousands of other visitors throughout those weeks, will ever forget Avedon's artistry. There were sensitive portraits of Marian Anderson, Truman Capote, Allen Ginsberg, Marilyn Monroe, Winston Churchill. Interspersed with the photographs were quotes from the master himself, revealing his crisp philosophy of life. I was touched by some shots of his father that apparently the senior Avedon disapproved of. As Avedon explained, he was more interested in catching surface than plumbing depth. It allowed vanity to suffer, of course. But it was the way Avedon thought people should allow themselves to be represented. Anything else was conjecture.

Near the beginning of the showing I was struck by a stunning portrait of Nureyev. His leonine hair at the ceiling of the frame shook the room alive. But his face! His face was full of the most fantastic zeal for life that I could imagine. His smile pounced out at me. The lines around his mouth said, in a hundred languages, "I love you." I became ignited. There was no escaping the sunny magic of this beautiful man. My eyes ran over the portrait in great circles, pulling out of it every fleck of black and white that composed Nureyev's countenance. Of a sudden my spirits bolted up from despair to elation. It happened. Just like that. It happened. For the first conscious moment in my life I was aware that my experience was one of man loving man. Call it what you will . . . fraternal, platonic, im-passioned. I knew. It was more than that. I knew.

. . . and pray.

lift up your hands

. . . and pray.

lift up your head

. . . and pray.

lift up your cross

. . . and pray.

America, America

Sandstone. It was the falling star of the north. A federal minimum security prison sitting one hundred miles above the Twin Cities. An Afro-American group there had banded together in a show of loving solidarity despite the procedural limits imposed by the federal staff. Their goals included studying African languages and history, mathematics, and politics, in the hope that they could help each other reach a keener awareness of the world around them. Officers were elected and the leader was called the Prime Minister.

It was Friday evening. The Afro band played a fast set and then the Minister of Recording, Watusi, gave the minutes of the last three meetings. It was near the anniversary of Martin Luther King's birthday and each speaker tonight would refer to it. But there was one speaker. There was one. He was ready and he laid it out. His name was Clarence Banks. I had never seen him before. His blackness was in a small wiry frame. He had notes but seldom looked at them. His voice came out slow and charged with a unique brand of dark soul.

Earlier today we paid homage to Dr. King. Although I hear the sound of a different drummer, I respect this man. Therefore I choose to honor all those that died because they were black. In lieu of a eulogy, my question is: IS THEM NIGGERS DEAD YET?

Does this question sound strange or foolish to you? Do you think this question too absurd to ask? If you think that white America is not waiting for an answer, you had better awaken. Blackness, like you, is the shadow of guilt that hangs over the conscience of white America.

He barely cleared his throat, now aware that his audience was with him.

There is a problem and we are it. Emancipation could not erase all the sorrows and cruelties of slavery. Liberty did not root out prejudice, and the carnival of blood and passion was too enjoyable for the evil men of this nation to really wish our black folks to be free.

So what came about was THE PROBLEM. Theirs. And with their limited desire for understanding and compassion, the only solution was genocide — the systematic killing and extermination of a whole people. I do not believe that the idea of genocide was premeditated. But the very nature of slavery, with its corrosive properties, would evolve into and contribute to the extermination of our entire race. Darkly, as through a veil, the faint revelation of what was being done came into the conscious mind of men without morals or conscience. And from that day to this, it has been their grand design to get rid of THE PROBLEM.

For two centuries before the emancipation, there was systematic and legal defilement of the black woman. This red stain of bastardy was meant not only to pollute and stamp out our African race, but to corrupt the moral fiber of chastity and bring about the obliteration of the family unit. The deadweight of this degradation fell physically on the black woman . . . but on the very soul and being of the black man this burden was also felt. For it was he who had to stand and watch with shackled hands, while the shrieking cries of his woman were to ring unanswered in the chambers of his mind.

And whitey asked, IS THEM NIGGERS DEAD YET?

I was afraid to move a muscle for fear of disturbing the electricity in the hall. Next to me sat Joe Archie, the Prime Minister. He was a zombie with no audible sign of breathing. The room was timeless. No throat coughed. No shoe shuffled. No chair creaked.

At the conclusion of slavery the black man was in a different hell. Freedom wasn't free. He was faced with vast despair because freedom meant he had to enter into competition with white folks for his livelihood. Can you visualize such a situation? Slaves now free. Dirt poor. Without home. Without land. Without tools or money. This against white America? The very nature of things registered defeat. Humility versus barbarism. Ignorance versus education. Purity versus crime. And over it all . . . prejudice. The children of this newfound freedom stood at the dawn of self-consciousness and self-examination, alone in the land of the dollar.

In such an atmosphere of contempt and hate, not knowing who he was or what he was going to do, and through the organized humiliation of his manhood, the black man was totally lost in sickening despair. This situation would disarm and discourage a nation of gods, let alone men. Hate and helplessness must find an outlet, and so there came about the attempted suicide of the black man as a nation. Personal disrespect and mockery of his brother became the vogue. Boisterous welcoming of the worst of us and ridicule of our own was in. The lowering of ideals and self-devaluation became the unwritten word. Self-criticism gave way to disdain for everything black. We as a people were diseased and spiritually dying. And whitey said, IS THEM NIGGERS DEAD YET?

No . . . them niggers ain't dead yet!

For out of the ignorance and the darkness and the evil there arose some strong and some mighty. Those sisters and brothers showed the way to life and to a clearer perception of black responsibilities. They brought the realization of the meaning of progress. Through education we began to fight the clawhooks of conflict, and with inspiration we strove to out-distance doubt. With faith we sought comfort from vain questioning. Black folks slowly began unifying in blackness, developing in talents and spirit. White America looked on in disbelief and bewilderment. They looked on with hate and sorrow.

DAMN!! AIN'T THEM NIGGERS DEAD YET?

Could white America just ignore the blundering but determined struggle of her black citizenry? Could liberty and freedom be a reality for these strong and resolute people? Would white America let these people live?

No. No. A thousand times it is no.

For on the warm southerly winds the midnight marauders came riding . . . white-sheeted figures thundering, thundering in. And the most frightful cries were heard when they scattered and slipped back into sunken cradles of respectability.

Strange fruit hang from the poplar trees . . . and the rivers fill with non-breathing flesh.

And Emmet Till was killed.

Thundering. Thundering. And Medgar Evers was killed.

Thundering. Thundering. Thundering. And those three civil rights workers were killed.

And those four little black girls sitting in church, they were killed.

Then Malcolm was killed.

And on some lonely highway someone else was killed.

And then Martin Luther King, Jr.

And in some dark ghetto alley, another is killed.

Only the mothers know the names of all the others who were killed.

Maybe you next time . . . maybe me.

IS THEM NIGGERS DEAD YET?

No, whitey. WE AIN'T DEAD. NOT YET.

JESUS CHRIST. Your name will last

But the union signed on a poor cast

YA GOT A POOR CAST

YA GOT A POOR CAST

On the car radio, KDWB strained in. Pat Deamer would play it up full throttle when the sounds were familiar. In between she'd talk of clothes, politicians, and our evening at Sandstone Prison. Pat was skinny and black and beautiful and highly intelligent. The brothers up north loved her and her husky voice. She loved visiting with them and accompanied me on my trips there whenever she could get away from a modeling assignment. She was brought up in Louisiana and hated that state.

"I'm not one for church anymore. Louisiana turned me off. Right off! One Sunday we sat up front in the long pews. It was a Catholic church and we weren't so poor that we didn't have any finery. The priest was white. The parish was white, too. They tried to show their liberalism with two black altar boys. At Communion, the priest dropped a Host on the floor. One of the altar boys whipped down and picked it up with his tiny black fingers. I knew the family and I knew the kid felt honored to be salvaging the Body of Christ. 'Get your black hands off that, nigger!' As the priest spoke, he reddened. We got up and walked out. I've never gone back. Always wondered what that boy did with the Host. Probably dropped it on the floor again."

scratchin' of pen on a long yeller pad
clang
body of men layin' down law
clang
crowd shufflin' shoes
afternoon blues
traffic and whistles and soul food and booze
clang
man
you were in jail before you wuz born
clang
you were put down
inside of a crib
clang
kitchy koo . . . baby coo . . . pink an' blue
WHAT you hear
clang
what you HEAR
clang
clang
clang clang clang

STILLWATER

It might have been a book. Instead, it's just part of one. A part I hadn't intended to write, until one evening three friends challenged me during a highly emotional session.

"You're too cool. How could anyone experience all that you tell about and not show anger? It doesn't make sense to leave out the Stillwater thing. You've got to write about the prisons . . . be angry . . . tell it. Otherwise you're cheating us."

Stillwater represents to me most of the pain I had as a

public official. Even with a moderately rough childhood, I still had some naiveté toward law and justice. No matter how many examples of prejudice I observe or experience, each one still disarms and surprises me. I always think people are going to be fair and tolerant and maybe loving. My reaction to Stillwater might have been far out of proportion to the magnitude of the event. It *was* a gassing, not a murder. Yet I was puzzled and unbelieving when I saw my political peers justify in dishonor the treatment of nine stripped bodies. I hated to admit that ultimately nothing would be done for them. I'd envision the power of government and fantasize that it would be used for justice, only to realize that my mental exercises were hopeless idealisms. I might just as productively cut paper dolls from the parchment of the United States Constitution.

Indeed, I hate writing this section. It symbolizes all the bile that crept into the clean parts of my anatomy. I disliked some people then, and I don't want to dislike again, yet I'm about to. I was afraid then. I don't want to dredge up that fear again. The fear of foul actions, brainy lawyers, legislators, my own inexperience. Stillwater is many things . . . some anger, some testimony, some shameful events. But mostly it is about how people related to people — savagely, bitterly, thoughtlessly. It might have been a book.

Compared to Alcatraz, Stillwater is the Newport Jazz Festival. Cons in Illinois, Massachusetts, or Pennsylvania would call Minnesota "good time." But then, I can remember Loehle Gast, a Fargo friend, saying, "If I have a toothache, it pushes the war news on the front page into second-class importance." Stillwater State Prison was our toothache. Those problems in New York's city jail were bad, but to nine inmates gassed in our state prison, it was all troubles and hurts, and to them it was important. I don't think Stillwater was too important to anyone else.

Ever since gas guns were invented, a core of prison authorities have brandished them like toys upon lambs as well as wolves. In March of 1967, after a particularly dubious demonstration of gas-power, District Judge Robert Bakke made a court decision:

> It is hereby ordered that the new gas weapon known as chemical mace or weapons of like nature emitting liquid or tear gas or other caustic or irritating materials shall not be used as a means of inflicting corporal punishment upon an inmate of the prison who is effectively confined and subdued in a locked cell and whose actions present no threat to the security of the prison.

On August 21, 1969, guards inhumanely tear-gassed nine naked men in a manner that stripped from them the last frayed threads of dignity. No one guard was ever held accountable. And although the governor called for an investigation, the legislature held hearings, the Corrections Commissioner stated his regrets, and the Grand Jury met in private court, they all condoned that terrible act of 1969. Not one of them had the humanity to put his moral sensitivities ahead of pressure, politics, or public judgment.

Lt. Kamps, Prison Guard
August 21, 1969

At 12:15 A.M. on this date, I received a call from Officer Weber who was posted in Segregation. He reported to me that a very noisy disturbance, consisting of banging of tables, yelling, and whistling, was in progress in the unit. The disturbance reached the point where it could be heard in the Custody Office.

Warden Young was called and given this information. I was advised to go to Segregation unit and if the disturbance did not come to a halt I was to move all participants into Isolation cells and use tear gas. I entered the unit with Sgt. Ebert, Officer Jorgenson, Officer Williams, and Officer Victor.

Officer Weber reported that inmate Eubanks was the leader of the agitation. Eubanks was removed from Segregation and placed in Isolation cell #10. He was quite belligerent and physical force had to be used . . . . One gas-billy cartridge was also discharged in his cell. Inmate Mason was removed from Segregation and placed in Isolation cell #9. One gas-billy cartridge was discharged in his cell. The disturbance continued in intensity and the other inmates continued to yell and whistle. They yelled to be taken to the "hole." Inmate Turpin started a small fire in his cell . . . . Inmates Claybourn and Johnson were placed in Isolation cells #7 and #8 and one gas-billy cartridge was discharged into the entrance to those two cells.

Inmates Myles and Brewer were placed in Isolation cells #5 and #6 and one gas-billy cartridge was discharged at the entrance of those two cells. Reardon and Turpin were placed in Isolation cells #3 and #4 and one gas-billy cartridge was discharged at the entrance to those two cells. LaMere was placed in Isolation cell #2 and one gas-billy cartridge was discharged into his cell.

At this time we stopped moving inmates, although Pittman, Driscoll, and Busten were very loud. The noise diminished and no further transfers were made. All Isolation cells were opened and the disturbance was under control. The Warden was so notified. After a period of time I walked through the Isolation unit and a number of inmates talked to me. They indicated that the reason for the disturbance was the fact that they could not get a nurse to see them. Inmate Turpin had asked to see a nurse at 11:45 P.M. and Sgt. Peterson went to him and told him he would contact the hospital for possible treatment. When immediate treatment did not arrive, the disturbance started.

The record will show that [they] have been abusing the night procedure . . . . I found that the nurse has made 23 calls to the Segregation unit since July 5, 1969 . . . one call per month was the prior average. Officers . . . have heard the inmates talking at night, trying to decide which one was sick so that they could ask for a nurse. I also told Turpin that he has been seen repeatedly and there is no basis for his complaints of illness.

Reaction was immediate. My predecessor in the Human Rights Department, Frank Kent, was deluged with phone calls from protesting citizens. In time, Frank charged Commissioner of Corrections Paul Keve and Warden Jack Young with discrimination, on the basis that "these incidents constitute mistreatment of persons confined and therefore a violation of the Minnesota State Statutes on discrimination." Of the approximately 900 inmates at Stillwater, 150 were black and 80 Indian. Of the nine inmates gassed, 5 were black, 3 Indian, and 1 white.

A citizen's charge was also drafted in the Human Rights Department and signed by nine people, among them Dennis Banks and Clyde Bellecourt of the American Indian Movement:

We the undersigned . . . charge the Minnesota State

Prison officials with cruel and inhuman treatment and racial discrimination. On several occasions inmates were gassed, beaten, deprived of food, and refused medical care. The water was turned off in isolation cells thereby creating unsanitary conditions. We believe that these conditions happen continuously and the incidents take place because the inmates are black and Indian.

The governor ordered an immediate investigation and asked Ramsey County Attorney John Jansen to determine whether criminal charges should be brought. Shortly afterwards, Kent moved on to a prestigious position in Washington, D.C., so the Stillwater case came to a standstill.

I took office in 1970 and was briefed on Stillwater by Frank Kent and our department attorneys. Soon I was on the phone with Arnie Schoeller, assistant to Attorney General Douglas Head, welcoming his advice regarding Jansen.

"We want this case, commissioner. Bad! The A.G. wants it. The governor ahhh wants it. Call the Ramsey County attorney and have a quick meeting. Ahhh do you know his name?"

"Yes."

"John Jansen. Call him. Ahhh have him meet in your office. See where he stands with his ahhh own investigation. His are criminal charges. If he acts gun-shy, then ahhh I'd keep my file away from him. He's in tight with that Stillwater bunch. Ya never know . . . "

"Thanks, Arnie. I'll call Mr. Jansen today."

A few days later, Jansen met with us. When he was shown in, I felt sorry for the middle ground he was camped on. We were four strong in number and I wouldn't have traded off. We sat in straight back wooden chairs, hand-me-downs from a condemned building. And we sat in a circle, nothing between us except carpeting and cigarette smoke. My office had a large, old, round, wooden table. It was bare but for a thick copy of investigator Walt Jones's file, lying slightly off-center.

"Glad to meet ya, commissioner. Heard you were once with Dale Carnegie. Took the course some time ago."

When the preliminaries were over I thanked Jansen for the second time.

"Thanks for agreeing to drive out this way. We all appreciate it. I only recently was briefed on Stillwater. . . understand that you were doing your own digging in the interim between commissioners. Since criminal charges are more serious than ours, we are eager to know what your thoughts are — how it's going — does it look like the nine inmates have a case?"

Jansen looked at all of us slowly. He was a little over-weight, had a warm and kindly face, and his hands and feet showed signs of nervousness.

He began, "I dunno. The guards have a point here. It's difficult to assess criminal charges when so many . . . so many . . . you know . . . when so many tensions are built up — on *both* sides. Public opinion and misunderstanding. It makes it difficult."

My heart fell out of its protective sanctuary. For the next half hour I peered through a window. The office was partially below ground level and my eyes could skim across stalks and weeds growing up to the building, a trap for scraps of paper and cups and other debris. Words from the group, the rubbing of wool on wooden chairs, a match igniting . . . all slid into my awareness as quiet intrusions and muffled vibrations off in the distance. I was in a reverie, no longer caring about Mr. Jansen. I was strumming time, lost in a detachment of minutes and space, hibernating until the meeting died a prolonged death.

Jansen was leaving. I heard him express disappointment at departing without the file. Someone said, "We'll think it over."

Then I was alone in the office again. The chairs were in an uneven circle. The table, large, old, round, and wooden, bore a thick, brown file . . . slightly off-center.

Inmate James Eubanks and Conrad Balfour

"I was in Segregation. Turpin says he sick."

"Was he?"

"Now I can't say to THAT. He been in the hospital, ya dig. I know he was in THERE for thirty days. It's jus' rumor . . . he's in THERE with all them egg sandwiches and cookies; ready to talk down some DUDE. He don't do that, and they put him in the hole, ya dig. We went along with that. Like I say, he says he sick. When he calls for the doc the screws say okay. But it ain't okay 'cause no one comes, ya dig. So we beat the walls . . . . About two hours later Kamps and his men come in with tear gas and saps . . ."

"Excuse me, James. The guards enter from where?"

"They come in from unit 1. I'm at the other end of the hall, in cell 1 of unit 3. They walk all the way past the other dudes and all the way over to me. Now THEY all makin' noise too!"

"Who comes?"

"There's Kamps and Jorgenson and an Indian . . . a real bigoted bastard. And there were about four others. Kamps says, 'Come out of there you son-of-a-bitch!' and then somethin' to the fact that I'm a troublemaker."

"How could you come out?"

"They're shouting through a door with a glass front. There's a box there, and they puts in a key and then turns a wheel . . . between the door and my cell is an entry way, ya dig. My door slides open when they turn the wheel. Kamps tells me they gonna take me to the hole. I ask them why they don't respond to our calls for a doc. That Indian says, 'We don't give a fuck about that! Get your black ass out of there!' "

"Did you punch a guard?"

"No. No. There were too many of them. I knew they wanted to assault ONE of us . . . bad. They got those gas guns and saps, ya dig. We walk past the units down to the hole. They stop me in front of cell #10. Some of the cells are paired up. I mean they separate, but they pair up to an entry way. Then I'm told to undress."

"What did you have on?"

"A work shirt. You know, just like this . . . jean pants."

"Any shoes?"

"No. No shoes."

"Underwear?"

"Yah, I got shorts. I start to go into the cell with my shorts on and they say to take them off. Then Kamps say, 'Give me those goddamn glasses!' I tell him I been in the hole before and he ain't gettin' nothin'. I start walkin' into #10 and Kamps hits me on the head with his sap."

"How do you know it was Kamps?"

"He was directly behind me."

"Does it knock you down?"

"No. No. I put my hand in his belt and pull him into me, ya dig. I'm hittin' him low and he gets in one more. The others jump on down but there's not enough room for all of us in there. I throw my glasses into the commode, and everything stops. There's some shit in there, but they take 'em out anyway. I told them whatever they going to do, you can't do anything more, so do what you're going to do. At this point Kamps shot gas . . . it was a terrifying experience. I've never been gassed before. I laid on the floor, then I got up and put a blanket over my face. I threw up blood the next day. It was specially bad by the commode. The water in the bowl attracts gas, ya dig . . . . My caseworker, Dick Steiner, he was there four days later. His eyes were watering and his face burning and he couldn't stand staying there with me for more than a few minutes."

Testimony from the 1969 Investigation:

Lt. Kamps

Kamps: As far as I know they did not get clothes for the three days they were in there. Was that about it? Three or four days that they were in there?

Investigator Walt Jones: They were in there about six to seven days.

Kamps: Oh well, whatever, they were in there, they didn't get any clothes. And I would like to add that the fourth morning, I just got called every rotten name you could think of . . . and I didn't take any kind of action against any of them. They called me every dirty, low-down name a human being could be called . . . awful!

Inmate LaMere

Investigator: Did you throw defecation into a guard's face?

LaMere: Yes! I sure did! We had no tissue paper for a week! I couldn't even wipe my ass! They said we'd only stuff up the toilet! The goddamn water didn't even run!

When that screw came by I threw it in his face!
Investigator: Then what?
LaMere: I said, "Here's some shit! If I stink, you're going to stink with me!"

Reardon, Caucasian Inmate
They skipped me. I was in the cell with two others and they weren't going to take me. I wasn't actually making any noise or anything but I was interested in it cuz I felt that if I was sick I sure would appreciate someone calling the doctor for me. That's the only reason I had gone to the hole. I asked them if they would bring me down there.

C. Richard Knowles, Prison Chaplain
If I said we didn't have racist people in this institution I'd be saying something that would be super miraculous.

Jack Peterson, Social Worker
In here, racism is a way of life.

Inmate Brewer
So then in the middle of the night I hear them shooting gas again. They shot gas twice.

Inmate Johnson
... about three o'clock in the morning they opened the door and Turpin still asked the man, he says he still sick and he wants the doctor, and the man said we've been pretending we've been sick for six weeks and all we want to do is for you to shut up, ya know. If you don't shut up, we'll give you some more gas. Then they gassed us before they left anyway.

Ted Lawrence, Social Worker

Gas does some terrible things. When the prison population goes to their daily tasks in the morning, they must walk past the section where Isolation and Segregation are located. The smell of the gas is then obvious to everyone in the joint. This has a deleterious effect upon all of them and in effect causes more tensions.

Associate Warden Alexander

. . . to me gas is a most humane way of handling any disturbance. You can say "why don't you use blackjacks and clubs," etc., but you can really give somebody an injury that they will carry the rest of their lives. And we are not out to do this . . . we had to gas them, to settle them down.

Our department hoped that Jansen would press criminal charges, because we had only discrimination to work with, and the redress there amounts to little. Ultimately, however, he did not move on the case, claiming lack of cooperation with the Department of Human Rights. In the meantime, I had ample opportunity to visit the black self-help group at Stillwater.

They met weekly to air grievances, discuss bylaws in their constitution, and share rhetoric with invited speakers. There were usually about sixty blacks in attendance and five or six whites. The rows of men seated in stiffly creased suntans and black shoes with white socks looked like a massive jury facing elected officers whose words and actions were ever on trial for integrity.

Sometimes I was seated off to the side, away from a direct line of scanning and piercing eyes. The chair to my right, a witness seat, was always taken in turns by men who desired to whisper a confidence. As one finished, he would slip off and another would take his place.

"My name is Bob Love. I want you to see my mother."

"Where does she live?"

After I wrote the address, he left and another sat down. The voice was low and barely audible. Both of our heads were leaning and meeting above the armrests between us. His voice murmured and the weight of his words tilted all of his body away from the plumb line. Our centers of gravity met outside our individual frames. He was the confessor in the confessional, pebble-low tones droning out personal pain. His head, shrouded in black, moved in delicate response to the slight nodding of mine. We were fronds of palm touched by the slightest of air currents, the stalks of our bodies rigid and still, the leaves in a motion of harmony . . . less than a dance, more than a roaring crowd.

He touched my hand, then drew away. The secrets were mine and he was gone.

Jack Peterson

He would usually send me a note. Maybe get on the phone. Stillwater was intolerable for him, his family, his education, his love of nature. A counselor with a master's degree was a rarity at the prison — a prison that cared little for any of his sensitivities.

"Connie, I hope you can do something. I'll believe it when I see it."

I had a green Grand Prix and we were sitting full slump inside it at Como Park. Ducks were walking the water line, a common focal point for our eyes, they as safe from us as the institution was from reform.

Jack intruded on my thoughts: "They treat 100 percent of the prison population alike . . . like they were all psychopathic murderers. Beat 'em down. Never let up.

The men — most of the men — can be helped. But they don't try to help. And if we try, one of us, we're treated as crazy people, as traitors, just for trying! I'm sad. They built the Segregation unit at half a million dollars and the warden is proud of it. Later they built a gym."

"I know," I echoed. "The guys that go to the hole — for what? A pin-up in the cell or a piece of bread snitched from mess. Lawrence says a guy was holed six months for cursing at a guard."

"I know that person," Jack said. "He's had a problem and maybe, I dunno, maybe we could have helped. He's sworn at me too. I'll tell ya, though, he's welcome to visit my home when he's released. Did Lawrence talk about our offices?"

"Yes," I replied. "Prison cells. The guards would lock you in them, pretending they didn't know they were occupied."

"My God! We'd have to wait for someone to let us out. I don't know why we put up with it! They dehumanize you! A few years ago a psychopathic inmate was constantly kept in the hole. If someone made trouble they would let George out into the population. They'd inform him that the troublemaker had called George a snitch. George would hunt down his victim with giant fists or a knife. He was deadly. When the victim was mutilated then George was put back in Solitary for punishment — until the next time."

Jack Peterson was my friend, but he never had friendly subjects to talk about around me.

It was the summer of 1970. I was invited to speak to the black self-help group at Stillwater. A tape recorder rested on the seat next to me. A guard stood near the door. The room was normally a visitor's section. Tonight it was converted into a town hall. I spoke with anger. I swore at the system that denied so many dignity. I cursed the handful of guards who made life miserable and intolerable for hundreds of inmates and a score of employees. I promised them I would do nothing to shame their faith in me. It was a violently angry talk.

It might have been the next day or two. I received a registered letter from Corrections Commissioner Paul Keve. He had dictated a well-worded, smoothly flowing document that until further notice banned me and members of my department from entering the institution.

Both of our offices, Paul Keve's and mine, were in the same building . . . Corrections on floor three, Human Rights in the basement. I thought kindly of Paul Keve. I think that he liked me. I thought him eloquent and bright, cautious and clever, humane and political. He might have viewed me as impetuous and bewildered. He must have wondered how I boxed myself into controversy. We were adversaries, yet he was never unfriendly, nor did he lose his composure. I sensed that down in his gut he was on my side. I'd stumble through a gripe, words tumbling out in disorder and confusion, and Paul would feed them back to me without any sign of one-upmanship or hint of superior sophistication. He would look into the distance, always a hair short of the remedy he needed to resolve a problem. I dealt with the emotion and passion of racism, he with the enigma of it. Somehow all the answers were "out there" for Paul and he was puzzled at their evasion. For me it was "in here" and I was frightened at their seclusion. To both of us the solution was equally invisible.

He would look at me, his head bald and his face grave.

The cigar, fat and long, warmed each word as it passed from cerebrum to mouth. When he spoke the white smoke pillowed his sentences so that they never fell heavy or touched down hard.

His memos; his letters; they moved with ease and calmness. When Paul banned me from visiting Stillwater, his letter had a tone of forgiveness. I belted out my hurt and anger and stormy rhetoric to sixty men . . . he poured in steady measure a warm ointment of prohibitive announcement.

The Senate Subcommittee on Corrections was scheduled to hold a hearing soon on the Stillwater case, and for this meeting, Paul wanted my help. "I want changes as much as you do, Conrad. I hope you can tell the subcommittee everything that you know to be shameful. I think it can help us all."

I spoke to the subcommittee for about three hours. At the end, Paul stood at the brown lectern and assailed me. Paul was a political man.

The Subcommittee on Corrections

At 9 A.M. I appeared at the hearing room. The committee was sitting in a square U arrangement, with spectators and press closer to the walls. I noticed Keve, Warden Jack Young, Mogelson of the prison union, and some guards. It was a tense setting.

Most of my remarks focused on inmate and guard testimony. I talked in machine gun staccato. The interruptions were frequent.

Senator Nyquist: Limit your remarks to references of discrimination, if you please.

Senator Brown: Commissioner, how can it be discrimination when one of the gassed inmates was white?

Paul Keve: Very unsubstantiated, inane, and none too tasteful.

Jack Young: The commissioner's remarks have covered a lot of areas and many innuendos have been made about many people.

Ex-convict: There is no discrimination in Stillwater.

At the lunch break I walked out of the room and down the massive capitol steps to the street below. I almost imagined that this was the Basilica Church I had so often attended; the great dome, the steps to the street, the empty feeling in my stomach. I heard running footsteps and turned. It was Senator Perpich. He was from Iron Range country and during the session he had asked sensitive questions that indicated understanding and empathy.

"Commissioner! Hold up! Hi. Say, you're getting the crap kicked out of you. I hope that you still hang in there. I don't know what I can do to help. They've just about made up their minds anyway."

He was a welcome ray of encouragement. Never in my life had I felt so discouraged, so lost. And frankly, I didn't want to return to that room.

After lunch as I waited for the meeting to resume, Mogelson, the union representative, said, "You are doing a terrible thing here. You will always regret it."

One of my attorneys seemed to avoid me. He sat in the back and during recess never said a word to me.

I went on for another half hour. At one point a committee member asked me when I would stop harassing the prison officials. In an explosive retort, Perpich, who was waiting for an opportunity to declare his frustration, burst out with, "When they stop discriminating in that place!"

After I finished, the chairman asked for responses. It was incredible. I sat there with my face aflame and listened to supporters of Stillwater and those who felt I was harassing blue-chip citizens, as they filed up, one by one, in a gray line of righteousness, to put the lid on Stillwater and its dirt. Everyone got their hands dirty. It was a very grubby day.

The staff had left for the night. Down the hall a black woman was sweeping the floors. On my desk were letters to be signed by the commissioner. One was to Warden Jack Young, another to Associate Warden Stanley Alexander, another to Lt. Gordon Kamps, informing them that the case was now closed. I signed them below the "very truly yours."

There were nine other letters mocking each other . . . all identical but for the name of the addressed individual:

Mr. _____
Stillwater Prison
Dear Mr. _____

Enclosed find a copy of the Hearing Examiner's findings. Thank you very much for all the cooperation you have given to this department. My very best to you.

Sincerely yours,

Conrad Balfour
Commissioner

I signed them with a shaking hand. My glasses had slipped down on my nose and my back ached. The door to my office was closed. I was crying and I knew that the cleaning lady would enter at any moment. Goddamn it! What was I signing! It was all so impersonal! The governor! Impersonal! The attorneys! Impersonal! The legislature and the commissioners! It was all so lousy! What the hell was I doing? What kind of protocol was this? How could anyone receive this trash? How could those nine inmates know that I haven't just written them off like so many of the rest? I imagined Johnson taking his mail from a uniformed man. Brewer sitting on his bunk opening the envelope. LaMere mouthing the printed words. Claybourn serious looking. I saw Mason and Myles cursing and Turpin crumpling the stationery.

God! God! Forgive me for spitting out the bread. Oh my God!

I think I placed my hands over my ears. I didn't want to hear my sobs. I wanted Reardon to know. Eubanks to know . . . to understand.

Lois Peterson: Eulogy for Jack Peterson, 1973

Yes, I loved my husband. He never had to doubt that. He worked in that sad building and tried to keep it from getting to him. Jack was there in 1968. In May of 1970 he was forced to resign. He tried to bring the prison into the twentieth century but they had only two staff meetings in two years. He was told, "You got to go slow on the throttle." George Crust, one of the very fine guards there, told Jack that he was expecting too much too soon. I'd talk to him, too . . . tell him he was bucking a brick wall. But he wouldn't listen.

Sometimes we'd snuggle at night and he'd share the day. That's when I'd get the angriest. Like the time he said Mr. Telander of the Parole Board told an inmate, "No parole this time. You haven't taken advantage of our training classes." A few months later the inmate returned and Telander said, "You're a pretty fickle guy. You've been in too many courses."

Jack was upset by the Parole Board's foul language. And

it would rankle him to see guards censor mail. *I'd* get so angry I'd want to call *somebody* — the governor or Paul Keve. But I guess we thought they wouldn't have done anything.

They had a vacuum cleaner there. The Parole office and Warden's office had carpeting, and it got regular cleaning. One of the case workers also had a rug but was constantly refused use of the vacuum. Finally Warden Young wrote a directive to take care of the rug. Associate Warden Alexander did. He destroyed it.

Jack was a creative man. He loved people. He would throw parties for fifty or sixty people. He'd always bring somebody home for dinner. I always had to be prepared. Jack believed in the basic goodness and potential of all men and passed this belief on to me. He believed that if given a chance, every man wanted to and could do good. He believed in the dignity of the human soul and spirit.

Our children Jeff, Scott, and Karen are nine, eleven, and thirteen. Before they were three he had them on canoe trips. We marveled that he could take us on a week-long canoe trip, following a wilderness map, and never make a wrong turn. But we teased him because he never fully mastered the right turns of city driving.

Jack and I grew up in Cloquet. This year would have been our twenty-fifth high school reunion. Jack would be forty-three years old on April 2. He kidded that he missed being an April Fool by one day.

After Stillwater he worked in a poverty program. Phone calls to his supervisor warned that he was a radical and a troublemaker. He had to quit. Then he was hit with all the phony turndowns. "Too establishment; too old; not a minority; overly qualified; not a woman." He tried factory work. This time he lied about his education. Said he was a high school dropout. They did a check and found out he had his master's.

From July of 1972 he was unemployed. I teach reading at Park High in Cottage Grove. That has helped. We've always wanted to sell this place . . . maybe get a resort. His friends would have helped, but Jack never felt right about borrowing money when he wasn't working.

He was in good spirits Friday morning. Friday was always special. When I got home we'd have a drink and talk and review our dreams. When he was depressed I'd know, because things didn't get done around the house. He was a better housekeeper than I am. This Friday he wasn't there. I saw that he had upholstered a footstool and had hung a driftwood mobile and an abstract painting he had redone. But I noticed the floor wax was out. And though the dishwasher was unloaded it wasn't closed. That wasn't like Jack.

That night he didn't come home. We had been married twenty years and only once before had he not come home. That time he was at the Leamington Hotel for a counselor's meeting. He was beaten up by three Indians and fell into an open elevator. Two Indian women found him and saw that he got to General Hospital.

And now he was away again. Saturday morning at 10 A.M. the police called. It was February 24. Jack had taken his old red convertible and crossed the Stillwater Bridge to the far side of the St. Croix River. At a spot that he and the children often visited, he parked and shot himself in the head with a deer rifle.

The neighbors are unfriendly to us here. All but the lady next door. I want to sell this home. It has four and one-half acres, but I want to sell. I'd be pleased if the family was black.

FALL

At the last moment I was invited to meet Father Hesburgh of Notre Dame University. He was the featured speaker at a Fighting Irish alumnae meeting held at the Town and Country Club of St. Paul. I arrived while dinner was in progress. My host saw me at the door and escorted me past the head table to a spot in the center of the banquet room. Walking past the dignitaries, I was acknowledged by Governor LeVander, St. Paul Mayor Thomas Byrne, Father Hesburgh, and others. Following dinner and Hesburgh's talk, I was making my way toward the exit when Mayor Byrne stopped me and we chatted awhile. I kidded him about an incident that had occurred two days earlier. At a human rights seminar he was trying to speak over the microphone but was muscled out and over by a black militant, Matthew Eubanks. Byrne would not give in and finally Eubanks retreated. I had admired the mayor for his courage so I took this occasion to say, "How does it feel to get pushed around by one of my brothers?"

Mayor Byrne laughed and replied, "Where were you? I needed ya, fella."

Suddenly a powerful voice intruded: "What are we going to do about a commissioner who is destroying the Department of Human Rights!!"

Stunned, I looked toward the voice and discovered the governor bearing down on me.

"What are we going to do about all the legislators who tell me that we have GOT to do something about the commissioner?"

I said something inadequate, I don't remember what, because I had lost my composure and could make no intelligent response.

"As long as I am governor of this state, there will never be a homosexual on my staff!" His voice was booming. I was still in shock. "And as long as I am governor of this state there will never be legislation to protect such people!"

I said, "I'm sorry, sir. I wish you wouldn't feel that way."

The governor's voice, in full-brimmed tonality, continued. "Why don't you spend your efforts on the things you have legal rights to explore? I have a drug committee. They don't waste their efforts on other issues! What do you think you're doing?"

"What committee do you have that protects homosexuals, governor?"

How many spectators there were to this affair I had no idea. I was so stunned by the public attack that I had no awareness of people around us. Mayor Byrne, whom I had forgotten was still present, said something about his city hall peers and a broken confidence. He thought it applied to this argument.

The governor went on about the embarrassment my department had caused him. I got angry.

"You can't even admit that homosexuals exist!"

"Of course they exist," he said. "So do prostitutes and criminals and drug addicts!"

"Governor! I hope that your grandchildren grow up free of this life-style. If they are not so lucky, then they can announce to the world that you don't give a damn!"

He measured me with his frosty eyes, then backed up and bumped into Wes, his bodyguard. They walked out to a waiting limousine.

Someone had his arm on my shoulders. It was Father Hesburgh. "Good luck to you, commissioner. God bless you."

Mayor Byrne focused before my eyes. He was surrounded by three very attractive women. "Connie. Call me next week. I'd like to have lunch."

"Fine. What will we discuss?"

He said, "Well, I don't want any of those homos calling on me."

I never called him.

W e started out on the road at noon. It would be a five-hour drive and a late return. Cass Lake had a fair-sized Indian population and Chuck and Charlotte wanted to share with me some of their memories of the place. We talked non-stop every mile of the way.

That evening we attended a business meeting at the city hall. Chuck gave a spirited talk on behalf of two Chippewas who had a complaint to bring against the town fathers. It was a lively and frustrating meeting. Afterwards, we drove the streets of town, saw simple Indian dwellings, heard local tales, then headed out to the highway in the shrouded night.

"Over in there we fished. Got some beauties. Too dark for you to see the water. The rice was once thick in there, but it's thin these days."

Chuck's burly body barely fit behind the wheel of my car. He was lost in some far-off and distant story that one day I would ask about. The dash threw up a quiet green that slightly illuminated his craggy face. He was reliving boyhood and it was delicious and sad. Charlotte was drifting into half-sleep in the back, occasionally murmuring some throaty response to Chuck's words.

He never stopped. For five hours he played out the story of the north. I listened and I heard. In the security of that Fisher frame I became his brother. His Indian face was the face of my father and nothing in the universe could harm me. And she, stretched out in back, protected us from evil spirits and white ghosts. The treble of her nasal membranes. The bass of his throat. Her whistling snore. His drone. The engine and the singing tires on the road. All the sounds. They nestled to my jacket and to my pants. They slid into my shoes and wound around my toes and kissed my arches. They rubbed and rolled up to my skin and caressed me. I knew who I was and how I was feeling. I was Indian. That night I was Indian. I felt the cover of sadness tucking me into my Indianness.

Never again would I pledge allegiance to a flag. The stars symbolized grand larceny . . . each five-pointer evidence left at the scene of the crime, each stripe a devastating horizontal of lands plundered and breasts bloodied. Oh how the squinted eyes must tear when Old Glory is unfurled — to the conquerors a surge of pride, to the conquered a tale of horror. How many plains are they buried under? How many wayside historical markers interrupt scenic routes with weeping inscriptions? Oh God! Stand ready to request Indian forgiveness. Humanity is not God enough to cry enough, to care enough. You must. Oh, I love you. I love you. I am Indian and I love you.

ooooohhh ya

ooooohhh ya

singin' the slipper man blues

C hannel 4 belongs to the people of the Upper Midwest. It is their channel. They love the homey style and the bald weatherman and the lack of slickness and the sports. But more than all that, they love Dave Moore. Dave had acting experience before he got into television. He knows his way around people and makes it pay off in news reporting. WCCO news features Dave as its anchorman and he is gold to the sponsors.

His voice is comfortable but never glib. His hair gray but just like Dad's. His face strong and yet with a wee bit of puffiness. You believe him when he slides into an editorial comment. He is always believable, no matter what the subject. Still, somehow, he rarely does commercials. It's as if he is being saved to hawk the great product up in the sky. He did for a time have a late news show called "Bedtime Nooz" that took advantage of his wonderful sense of comedy. Sealy mattresses were riding the crest of popularity when Dave decided to call it quits.

Once he returned from a vacation with a full mustache. The station drowned in a flood of mail resenting his change of image. It wasn't that folks didn't appreciate a well-trimmed upper brush. It was just that Dave was special and timeless and solid for all of them. They needed

him to be there when they wanted a friend . . . right
THERE, at 10 P.M. . . . to tell them what was right and
wrong in the world. And they wanted Dave with his puffy
neck and slipper voice and gray hair just the way he was
the night before.

Dave was going to shave the darn thing off anyway.

When a filmstrip would show the wounded and dead in
Vietnam, or a fire in Philadelphia, or a killing in Columbus, the returning camera would catch Dave with a look of
concern, or disapproval, or wonder, or pain. He often told
me that it was not good policy for him to wear his editorial
looks and he would try next time to appear neutral. But
next time the camera would catch him again with torture
in his face or tears behind the eyes or judgment on his
brow.

He felt guilty around me. He always thought that I was
doing meaningful things to help the world, while he
merely reported the efforts of important mortals. Dave
would praise me and others and wonder how we kept
going in this screwed-up universe.

One afternoon at the YMCA I had just finished a tough
paddleball series and cold-showered until my skin called
out in sheer happiness. I ran into Dave coming down the
outside stairs for his daily workout. He was looking down
at the floor as he always does, and I called to him twice as I
always do. He looked up slowly and from seriousness to a
wide grin he greeted me with special fervor.

"Hi, Dave. I caught you editorializing again last night. It
was beautiful."

"I did? What did I do?"

"It was a network filmstrip. The announcer talked about
how little it matters what politicians or presidents say

about war. The killing still goes on."

Dave nodded, "Yah, I remember. I've got to stop that. It's no good to show my feelings. Ya know Connie . . . I wish I could do what you're doing."

He walked toward the locker room, his chin toward the floor again, his back hunched, a sad figure, bearing all the cruel news of the ticker tape world on his loving shoulders.

58

DECEMBER

It was idle time. For me that's picking up a book. Any book. This was a hardbound historical on Stephen Collins Foster.* It had great sketches of the Mississippi and the cotton gin and the old home down south, and the music and lyrics of his best-loved songs. I became very interested in Foster. Every so often an event in his life would remind me of a black slave boy whom a hoary old minister told me about one evening. The boy's name was Benjamin Davis. Benjamin Franklin Davis.

Stephen Collins Foster was born in Lawrenceville, Pennsylvania, now part of Pittsburgh, on the Fourth of July, 1826. At the very moment he was taking his first breath, his father was toasting the nation's independence in a local meeting place: " . . . our venerable progenitors . . . bequeathed [to us] the dear-bought inheritance; . . . and the most sacred obligations are upon us to transmit the glorious purchase, unfettered by power, to our innocent and beloved offspring."

No one remembered what day Benjamin Franklin Davis was born. His mother knew it was a day close to that Sunday morning. She had carried the basket of clothes to

*A Treasury of Stephen Foster. Foreword by Deems Taylor, Historical Notes by John Tasker Howard (New York: Random House, 1946).

dry out on the line that clung from the stake to the shed. She wondered if the weight of the wet laundry would this time pull down the shed wall. All at once her ears exploded: Glass! Rocks! Wood! Screaming! The Tyler Street Church had blown up!

"Away Down Souf" — Foster, 1848

Of eleven children, Stephen was the tenth. His dad was once a mayor, and a brother was successful enough to become the vice-president of a railroad. One sister even married the brother of President James Buchanan. Stephen, more than any other family member, loved music. In order not to shame the family by overindulging in song alone, he joined his brother in a business at the age of twenty.

Benjamin Franklin Davis never knew his dad. Once he asked his mom about a picture that stood on the hard table next to the bed. The man wore a field hat that shielded the light from a black face. The eyes shone from the black with a wet brightness. The nose was flat and roofed a fiery black mustache. His mom said that he was just a friend.

"If You've Only Got a Moustache" — Foster, 1849

Stephen was a capable bookkeeper. He still loved music and bandied his time with minstrels, hoping they would sing his works. "Oh! Susanna" and "Old Uncle Ned" were pirated from him by unscrupulous acquaintances. W. C. Peters, a music publisher, accepted some of Foster's works and made himself a fortune. Foster gained fame if not money. "Oh! Susanna" became a sensation. Minstrels sang it constantly, as did the forty-niners on their way to California. Two publishers offered him future royalties. He now knew that he could show to his family that music offered him a better future than book-keeping.

Davis heard about the cities back East, but to him it was only a dream. He loved to sing in the fields, or to hum in the fields, or if he had just swigged the liquid, to whistle in the fields. Yes, he loved music. His mom loved music, too. Everyone loved music, he told himself. Black people talked music as much — as much as they talked talk. Davis wasn't certain what song he loved most. His mom seemed to favor "Glory to the Master," but he was inclined to let his mind turn over a new tune he had heard a visitor singing.

"Oh! Susanna" — Foster, 1848

Stephen married Jane McDowell and proceeded to compose his finest songs:

"Old Folks at Home" in 1851
"Massa's in de Cold Ground" in 1852
"My Old Kentucky Home" in 1853
"Jeanie with the Light Brown Hair" in 1854
"Come Where My Love Lies Dreaming" in 1855
"Gentle Annie" in 1856

This gave him a fair income but certainly not wealth. In six years he earned about ninety-five hundred dollars.

Davis had a beautiful voice now. The richness and huskiness made other field hands stay their voices in deference to the younger man. Lord how the day seemed to be God-delivered. Even the master took on a kind face when Davis would sing. Many a wise head considered him a fancy catch. Some day the master might let him select a wife. There was no need to think complaining thoughts. After all, Benjamin Franklin Davis was richer than most.

He had steady employment and a place to rest his head. Better still, he had his mom. Next year would be a rich year, even better. Thirty-six dollars! He didn't want to think about it. THIRTY-SIX DOLLARS!

"Hard Times Come Again No More" — Foster, 1855

Stephen started on bad times. His music seemed to lack the warmth and richness of earlier days. Yes, it was true that "Old Black Joe" was an inspired work, but of one hundred tunes, it was the single flash of brilliance. Firms were delighted to have his name in their catalogs despite the absence of worthwhile work. Foster spent his income as fast as he received it and mostly on alcohol. He soon became incurable. Jane tried to help but it became more difficult. At times they would separate, Jane keeping their only child, Marion. Finally she had to leave Stephen for good.

Sometimes Davis would have a great longing for a woman. At night he would sit in a corner by the woodbox and fondle the black crock jug that often held his dreams. He sipped the liquor, always slowly, his hands and fingers sliding over the crockery arousing him more than the fluid. Maybe a woman felt as pleasant. Had someone fondled his mom this lovingly? Was it the friend in the picture? Davis noticed that his own skin was a lighter brown than either one of them. The clear whiskey made him burp. A tiny burp. He'd need sleep now. Beautiful sleep.

"Why, No One to Love?" — Foster, 1856

A friend received a message to come to the hotel. Stephen was on the floor, his neck on a piece of broken crockery, bleeding from a long black cut. A doctor sewed him up with black thread. In the hospital he wakened only to return to a black coma. At 2:30 on a Wednesday afternoon, January 13, 1864, he died in his sleep. His possessions were coat, vest, pants, hat, shoes, overcoat, and thirty-eight cents in coin. There was also a slip of paper that said, "Dear friends and gentle hearts." These belongings are now preserved at the Foster Hall Collection of the University of Pittsburgh, together with a manuscript of his works.

It was Sunday morning. The master and his family were at church. Davis was breathing hard as he fondled the soft dark muscles beneath Angelina's shoulders. It was a long spell to wait for what a woman promised. His thoughts. His thoughts. All that was over now. Whoever came through those big doors was never seen by Benjamin. Angelina screamed — he remembered that. Then the pain! The redness! The blackness! Ahhh MY GOD! ... Davis was put to rest under the hill with his mother's friend. His only possessions were the clothes that had rested on the ground beside him.

"Angelina Baker" — Foster, 1850

two

It's a long ride back to suckle that breast . . .

Looooong way from home mom

    and feel like ta' die

Hope them teats don' never run dry

Don' never run dry

Don' never never never

      run dry

BOSTON

Once again, it was Christmastime, my favorite season — and one that always brings to mind those days
long ago when I was a kid in Boston. Boston was at its
finest in the twelfth month. I remember the narrow town
streets, some cobblestoned . . . the Old Granary Burying
Grounds . . . the Salvation Army's Santas tolling their
brass bells for silver coins . . . the parcels and packages
propelling pedestrians past each other blindly . . . the
throngs of jaywalkers bumping along . . . crisp night air
and blaring horns and pigeons bleating and fluttering after
popcorn and peanuts . . . all this and so much more
thumps my heart with gaiety and tinges it with sadness.

We were young, and we never got disenchanted with the
magic of the season. Gangs of us attended Midnight Mass
on Christmas Eve at the Cathedral of the Holy Cross. One
year, as we started out for midnight services, we walked
past a seedy barroom on Appleton and Dartmouth streets.
A lady with crutches came out and asked me to escort her
home. It was on the way and in spite of the hoots of my
friends I walked her to Union Park Street. She pumped
along at a fast pace, the rubbered wood planted out forward and the rubbered shoes hopping to keep up. At her
door, as I was about to take her arm and walk her up the
stairs, she bolted from my side, crutches held aloft in one
hand, and up the steps she skipped like a panicked duck. It

wasn't until Christmas Day that we learned she always went drinking with crutches — after last call for drinks, she used them to support herself as she wended her way home.

Louisburgh Square always made our Christmas Eve more special. It stood back of Boston's famous Beacon Hill . . . rows of brown-bricked houses, two, three, and four stories, all looking into garden earth within a black iron fence. Dozens of carolers, ourselves included, went from home to home in smaller groups, paused before each door, and sang merry music to the occupants who stood at their thresholds and led us in their favorite carols. Some supported candles whose tiny flames tried to break away from the blackened wicks, or held carillons with their chromatic scales tunefully challenging our untrained voices. Sometimes there was punch on a stoop or hot cider against a rail. We'd huddle and hunch our shoulders in the cold and permit our notes to emerge joyously beneath the trickles of runny noses. We'd marvel at particular doors that had brass knobs and hinges, or steps that wore iron boot scrapers. Now and then, with our boots we'd lift a heavy ring imbedded in the cobbled sidewalk, a ring that once held reins of snorting bays. And when we finished our melodic rounds, we'd shuffle off across the Public Gardens, past George Washington on his horse, past the still trees whose buds delayed their birth until after the borning of the man from Bethlehem.

It made no difference how much the city was in your blood. When they dumped their garbage out of a third-floor window, our ball game halted. At the Rice School, the center of activity, the focal spot, was always home plate. Behind home plate was a wall bordered by fenced-in yards that sprouted tenement houses whose windows spied in on us. So when they dumped garbage from one of those windows, it was damn difficult not to notice. First a third-floor window screen got pulled inside the apartment. Then a terrible man would lift a barrel, branded red with his personal markings, and pour that filth down into his yard. It was so incredibly sick — cans and chicken bones and wet paper and melon rind and Kotex showered in color and clatter to the stinking earth below.

It wasn't so much the filth. It was the desecration of a moment, of a ritual, that all of us held in sacred reverence. Some of us were giants. Super performers. Gods. Station 4 policemen never interrupted during league play. Rival gangs never crossed that line between the South End and the rest of the world. Radios never blared, and the *Record*, *Post*, *Globe*, and *Herald* were put aside until the last out. Every soul knew these things except that son-of-a-bitch on the third floor.

We called it New York Ball in some respectful salute to a city that had Yankee teams and immortal rosters. All life revolved around the summer pastime. At season's start, four captains would sit on the Rice School steps and carefully select the players. Every boy in the neighborhood was evaluated and drafted in descending order of skill. The greats were first to go: Beansy Bardho, Honey Shionis, Bullets Martin, Chuggy Davis, Jerry Purcell and his brother Jackie. Then the near greats, the pitchers, the average hitters, the no-skills, and finally, the under-age.

Nothing interrupted these nightly battles, these daily routines, except heavy rain or season's end. Gang members grew up in it from ten-year-old hero worshippers to fifteen-year-old fielding wizards. Troublemakers avoided Station 4 lineups to make the roster. Leaders emerged to command respect on the field, such as could not be duplicated in an iron-disciplined Armenian household or Jewish synagogue. We were good kids. Spitting, swearing, multiracial, good damn kids.

The ground was hallowed before our time. Great teams had fought wars here every year: the Bruins, the Wings, the Spiders, the Old Timers. We treated the field with respect and courtesy. One day before the first game of a twin bill, an adult announced to all, "I'm gonna take a piss." As he walked toward third base, Art Carr, big as a man, said, "You don't piss."

"I'm gonna take a piss," was the repeated announcement.

Art moved in with a green broom handle and gravely proclaimed, "NOBODY pisses here!"

The man grabbed both thighs as if to extract strength from those muscles, looked past Art to the shortstop waiting to continue warm-up pegs to first, said, "Yah. Well all right," then walked out of the yard forever.

Here was our chapel. Our temple. We sprained ankles here. Ripped pants at the knees and scuffed sneaker toes here. Here we lost small pieces of skin and pulled out splinters from our palms, wore each other's shirts, and collected quarter dues. We learned to respect children and each other. Some were leaders and others humble servers. Yet for us there would never be a monument like the great one in Yankee Stadium's center field. No article on page one of the Sporting News describing the Chiz's pitching feats. No Hall of Fame to perpetuate the Greek, the Albanian, the Dago. Who would remember any of us now? Or the balls flying across the water-green roof in center field, the colored bats leaning against the drainpipe near home plate, the umpire's primal cry of "SAFE" echoing through those fluted years? Who would remember? Who would know?

It was just a pick-up game: Saturday morning at the schoolyard. Some of us were hanging around when Ted Barco's gang came down and challenged us to some New York Ball. Short was my regular position, but when it was horsing around time I took my position at the mound. They had their first ups. One of the kids moved into the batter's box, but as he tried to take a stick from a teammate, he was refused.

"You not on the team, man!"

"C'mon! C'mon! Lemme have the bat, man!"

"No man! You not on the team!"

Prudence should have dictated that I mind my own business. Instead, I shouted to the maverick to get out of there and "let's get this thing on." In a flash he picked up an empty Pepsi bottle and flung it at me. I hit the ground belly-down on my hands, then sprung at him before the skittering sound of glass subsided out in right field.

My first punch was uncontrolled, violent, and lucky. It must have found his head for I saw him sink to his knees, his hands and arms reaching out to me, flailing to keep that balance between agility and loss of control. Now his arms circled my legs, pulling me toward the noise in his head, and as I toppled over onto him my groin felt the teeth digging through the blue bellbottoms and into my flesh. At first I pummeled at him in an attempt to loosen this human attachment, but it was to no avail. Finally I lay still, resigned to whatever would follow . . . an unreal sculpture of two forms in violent repose. Presently one of his gang shoved two fingers into his nostrils and yanked. Off he came. We crawled away from each other, back to our own sides. My gang walked away with me to a corner where we could assess the damage.

I pulled down my torn Army-Navy bells. My shorts had scruffed up in a roll to the top of my thighs, and there below my privates on the inner shank were the perfect impressions of human teeth.

"Geez, he just missed ya' balls!"

Charlie Androcopolous thought I should go to City Hospital. "You could get rabies. Human teeth is worser than animals'!"

At City Hospital a lady wrote something on a pink card before a bald orderly escorted me to a cluttered room and asked me to undress. He had me climb up on a stretcher where I slipped beneath a folded sheet. Every few minutes he would return, ask how I was doing, and assure me that the doctor wouldn't be too long. I was trying to close my eyes and work out a way to leave this place with pants that weren't torn at the crotch when the door opened and the bald head of the orderly walked over to me smiling.

"How ya doin'," I said.

"Fine, young fella. I'm doing just fine. But how are

you?" With that he thrust his hand under my sheet and patted my penis.

"Kiss off, you son-of-a-bitch! Kiss off!"

He backed away, looked into my eyes, then slightly shrugged his way out of the room. When the door closed behind him, I got up and put on my damp shorts and torn blues. Then I walked out of there back to my neighborhood, twenty blocks and a dozen worlds away from Boston City Hospital.

When I'm near to eighty-two

I'll save a piece of ass for you

Sonny boy

Sonny boy

She was across the street close to the brownstones, less walking than flitting toward the corner traffic light. Her gait must have been tedious, but to me it was an old woman almost blown along, like a scrap of paper turning and touching down from door to door. If the Boston winds had shifted she might have moved along with them to the opposite end of Columbus Avenue.

I don't know why I watched her. The avenue was a depository for pained transients. Bookies made paper hits here. Police cars pulled up to a crowded drugstore for the *Daily Record*. Gypsies sat darkly in storefront windows abandoned to them by businessmen long since gone bankrupt. Pimps and hoods pulled up to the 411 Bar in Caddies and Olds while prostitutes arrived in cabs. Old men shuffled to a store for Apple's chewing tobacco and old women carried tinkling milk bottles in linen shopping bags. But I watched her as she reached the corner and leaned against the brownstone building firmly, so as not to be blown any farther. The traffic light turned her color and she quickly pushed off from her perch as if to gain momentum for the journey across the street. She swung back up the avenue now, still close to the buildings, lurching against them at various speeds, apparently oblivious to any motive other than advance.

The brick partition that supported my body was between a pool hall and a bar, both with windows that slanted away from the sidewalk in a V that collected blowing papers and mounds of crusted dirt. Because of this angled architecture, the lady was forced to walk much of the time under her own power. As she came close I heard her gasp. The ancient larynx clacked the sounds of a witch throwing craps, and it could well have been snake eyes that fell out above the hollows of her cheeks.

She stopped before me. I felt that I was depriving her of a partition that was rightfully hers for support.

"Heh, heh. How old are you?"

There were no teeth. The face was one thousand years older than mine and her left cheek had a hole in it, partly covered with a fold of skin. She was white with white hair and white hands that showed watery blue lines stuck to skin and bone.

"I'm sixteen," I said.

Her eyes moved into mine and fixed us both to each other. She picked up the hem of her dress and twitched the rag in a gesture of coquettishness. Her sagging stockings came up out of black sneakers held up by the glacial-like movements of years of dirt. The voice spit out from the toothless cavity, "Ya wanna piece of ass? One buck."

She drifted to the corner, a part of the shadows on this side of Columbus Avenue. A cake wrapper . . . Devil's Dog Cake or maybe Hostess Cup . . . crackled in the street as the acrid city breeze pushed it along. I watched it come to a stop against the curb. When I looked up again, the lady was gone.

and her legs gone bad

and her heart gone bad

and her blood and her hands and her innards

gone bad

and her seein' and her hearin' and feelin'

real lean

but she don't smell coffin wood and her smellin'

is keen

she don't smell noooooo coffin wood

and her smellin' is keen

ROSELLA

Her rocking chair moved incessantly. Eee-yeek. Eee-yeek. I watched the runners lift up off the linoleum floor, then suspend and pause before descending again. The monotone rhythm caused a subconscious response within me. I'd catch myself raising and lowering my chin in cadence to it. The eee-yeek was not irritable. In fact, the volume of sound was low enough to dull the senses in pleasurable somnambulism. I'm sure it was that way for her also, Rosella Beckair, grandmother extraordinaire.

Brown slippers, old brown stockings, brown and blue dress and apron all blended into the warm wood of her whispering chair. How I loved her. Even then. And how I wished that I could tell her, "Mom (I called her Mom), I love you."

Of course, she knew that anyway. Everyone loved her and talked of her and clamored to meet her, or bragged to friends that they did know her. She was an old woman at peace with herself. She wasn't wise or blessed with special intelligence or a symbol of some envious past. She was a woman, and she loved people with intense fervor, and for that she became a ghetto legend.

Now her eyes were closed, the thin face looked puffy as she dozed, and the round cheeks held the drooping glasses from tumbling to her lap. A snore would sometimes tease its way from her nostrils, adding to the sleepy sounds of the rocking chair. There was no snap to her face. No sharpness. Just soft chocolate blackness. Warm, tender, embracing blackness . . . glowing, always glowing. When I looked upon her face I could feel good. I knew that thunder and turmoil and bogeymen were not in this room with us. She was peaceful in sleep, and I was peaceful, too.

Rosella was born in Kingston, Jamaica, the daughter of a proud, religious mother. She was the skinniest child in the village and the swiftest runner. Through some special responsiveness in her personality, Rosie was concerned with the comforts of the sick and aged earlier than most. If the supper hour found her absent, it was accurate to guess that she was tending someone who was ill or needy in the village.

This empathy in Rosie's West Indian soul in no way exempted her from harsh whippings and quick justice from a mother who demanded that her children have respect for elders, obey without question, and ask God to have mercy on their souls. But her mother also knew how to recognize opportunity, and when a proper gentleman of means came along, there was no gainsaying the merits of Rosie becoming his bride. Thus, in her teens, Rosella King became the tender, virgin wife of Mustaffa Beckair, Turkish restaurateur and entrepreneur. Four children later a banana ship moved the family to America. Sidney Beckair stayed behind in Jamaica, but sons Edmund and George and daughter Ruby landed in Boston around 1912.

Soon after, Mustaffa (in America he was called John) left Rosella and went off to other cities. Rumor had it that America's racism was too much for him to cope with. In time, the Beckairs became United States citizens, sorting out new directions to follow in a new country. George went West and worked as a black cowboy, Edmund got caught up in the rackets, and Ruby went on to college where eventually she settled into social work.

I came along in 1928, arriving as suddenly and mysteriously as Mustaffa had departed. Neither Mom nor Ruby offered any explanation, and no one else asked questions. I simply arrived as a full-fledged member of this proud family, and received all benefits that clan, caste, or tribe might proffer, except for the family name. Imagined or real, it seemed to me that I was told my father and mother were killed in a car accident. This at least provided me with a quieting statement for curious juvenile peers.

78 Middlesex Street sat at center block, the stage for Ostoposides on the third floor and Psomiades on the second to play out city sharecropping. There was always enough lamb, rice, and grapeleaves to go around for

friends, and with a grandmother who had learned to appreciate and prepare Turkish dishes, the tenement bonds grew fast.

There was usually a dog to take up a small boy's time . . . imaginative names like Rex and Spot and Wolf. Newspapers spread across the kitchen linoleum gave hint of hope that Spot would somehow learn to deposit his warm urine in the proper place. The wrath of Rosella was assured if that anticipated deposit misfired.

"Damn! Goooddamn it! What do YOU mean! You DON'T pee here! Do you understand? NO! NO! NO! You don't pee HERE! Next time I'll smash you! NOW, go away! GO AWAY!"

It might have only cowed poor Spot, but her admonitions certainly had full sway over me — I never wet my bed as a child.

Holding court in the rocking chair, awake or asleep, Rosella was the heart of the household, the nucleus of the neighborhood, the symbol of the South End. By week's end, streams of callers had visited, paid respects, and then departed, taking with them generous portions of life and growth.

Protestant ministers came and talked of the Old Testament, priests on attending the Cathedral of the Holy Cross, insurance salesmen with ten cent policies, Syrians showing suitcases of dress materials, children asking permission to play with me, Armenian gangsters with bags of groceries, gypsies to drink her homemade beer, Germans with homemade hot sausage, Irish bookies to play a number she had dreamed, suitors to impress her before dating her coveted daughter . . . they all came to talk and to listen to her tales of God and Jamaica and voodoo. The calypso accent and rounded cheeks were morning bells in spring. Her singsong voice provoked their laughter, and the obvious excitement she showed at their presence made their day more joyful.

Mr. Mueller would tease her about the faded old apron she folded her hands on. "Now, Mr. Mueller, you just quit that. I think you must want some young man to see me all decked out and ask for my hand in marriage." Then they'd laugh tears from their eyes until both were weak from their merry exertion. Helen McCready thought her daughter too flirtatious and Rosella would look grave. Apple (I only knew him by that nickname) would ask what she needed for her cupboard, and she'd purse her lips and say, "Why don't you see what the kind grocer feels I can afford." They came every day, Sundays included, and exchanged the gifts of their stature and means. You knew it was time to leave when the chair slowed perceptibly and her chin descended to her rosaried chest.

Mom's abilities as a seamstress were wanting. I remember swapping off between the two pairs of knickers she created. No one else at the Waite Elementary School wore such ugly apparel, but more dreadful than that was the simple architectural design of my fly. It was a mere opening covered over with a folding flap that had the untimely propensity to work open when I least needed its service.

As for cooking, she was a whiz at preparing old world dishes, exotic Syrian delicacies, or just plain old-fashioned soups. She collected various rocks and agates to place in the kettle with all the condiments and herbs delivered by boat from the old country. Her dumplings were morsels of early heaven, her puddings delectable beyond description. But fried eggs were hard and soft eggs too runny, chicken gray-skinned and pebbly, and pancakes sat in your stomach like granite. Having to eat American food motivated me to rare periods of rebellion, and these uncomfortable episodes ended with my banishment to bed.

She was also a master in administering to ills, no doubt a carryover from her childhood. One day I had a painful, hacking cough. Mom boiled an onion on our black pot-belly stove and made me drink the fuming liquid. Knowing full well that this concoction was going to kill me, I drank it down, cried, and then never coughed again.

Another time I was eating an ear of sweet corn in our basement before a drooling, soulful-eyed dog. I held the cob out to Rex and as he committed his snout to the succulent husk, I cruelly yanked it away. After the third or fourth time, Rex came at me and put his teeth into my skin just above the eye. Yelping pain and consternation, I roared upstairs to find Mom. She took one swift look at my bleeding face, and without saying a word, cleaned the wound with brown soap, applied a potion of green peas and human hair, and bandaged it all with clean cloth. Then I embarrassedly walked to City Hospital, where white-suited medics laughed and looked at each other before changing the homemade bandage with one of their own. Today I don't recall which brow I injured, for there is no tattling scar.

We had just a kitchen and one bedroom. I had my own bed with a tiny gray pee pot beneath it. (The cellar was too dark and foreboding for a little boy and too cold and dirty for adults to make use of the makeshift plumbing.) My grandmother and Ruby shared the larger bed; there were two larger pots beneath that. Most of the intimate lessons of life for me happened in this room. I first learned that women peed differently than I did when on occasion I indiscreetly came upon one or the other using a bed pot. I never saw my grandmother naked, but often Ruby would be in bra and panties, the pink material hardly holding back any of her femininity.

When I was about twelve, I would sometimes creep out of bed and sneak looks through the slightly opened kitchen door to watch Ruby bathe at the kitchen sink. Mom would chastise her for neglecting to pull the blinds, but Ruby was quite unconcerned about peeping toms, for once I saw her make an obscene gesture at an imagined voyeur across the alley. Only five feet tall, she had a devastating figure, a beautiful almost oriental face, and a sharp mind. I was confused by her sexuality and couldn't quite understand the quickness in my loins.

One night I was snuggled safely into my bed, the covers pulled up and around my back so that they came just under my ears. I had a way of resting on my stomach with my fingers hooking onto the blanket edge so that it stayed in place just at the base of my head. I felt particularly happy and, like Rex wagging his tail, I "wagged" my body side to side, up and down, in some primitive, ecstatic glide across the sheet. My thighs flowed in an easy, sliding, animal rhythm that I had never known before. Running freely across Emerald Street . . . propelling my scooter down the Hingham Street Hill . . . the coastal breezes airing Uncle Edmund's Oldsmobile on a ride to the Cape . . . none of these were as tingling to my body, none so stimulating. Somewhere beneath me was a giddy spasm. Then warm. Then wet. I rolled over to the side of the bed and pulled my pajama bottom over the pajama top. The wet couldn't touch my skin now. I pulled my legs up to my chest, tired and out of breath.

Mom: What shall we do?

Ruby: Nothing. He may have learned it in the Boy Scouts.

Mom: All we can do is pray for the boy.

Ruby: It's not good for a child to sleep in the same room with women.

Mom: All we can do is pray.

Peter Bent Brigham Hospital is world famous. Uncle Edmund insisted that Mom convalesce there when she became ill. I was told that she suffered from cancer and gangrene of the legs. Her sugar diabetes made it impossible to operate. I don't remember how long she was hospitalized, but eventually the doctors dismissed her to die in the peace of her home. Ruby said she only had days to live.

One morning I awakened to the murmur of Ruby and Mom talking in lowered voices. I sensed the religious quality of their discussion and kept my eyes tightly shut so as not to intrude.

"Wake Conrad," my grandmother said. "Conrad. Are you awake?"

Ruby approached my bed and rolled my leg under her hand. "Wake up, dear. Morning now."

I opened my eyes and squinted into the morning shadows, feigning the look of a young boy disturbed in his sleep. Ruby sat on my bed as I pushed myself to an upright position.

"I had a dream this morning," my grandmother said. She was reclining on her back. Two large pillows propped her head almost forward. She wore a white nightcap, the black face a dark pond beneath frozen foam. Without her glasses the eyes seemed darker and unopened. Slender hands embraced each other above the turndown of her sheet.

"I was in my bed. Suddenly Mama appeared standing here . . . next to me."

She neither pointed nor nodded toward the spirit-held place on the floor where her mother stood, but I knew all the same.

"Mama said, 'Rosie, don't be afraid. You will be fine.' Then she stretched across the bed — she touched both sides without touching me."

The stillness carried her quiet words. "Ruby, get me my slippers."

I watched them relating to each other, mother to daughter: the tiny, strong form of the young woman folding the soft covers back, embracing the long, bony legs of the tall, older woman, whose arm was around her daughter's shoulders, her narrow feet sliding into the fur-lined slippers. She stood . . . unsteady, but she stood. She knew she would be fine.

Ruby's arms enclosed the waist section of her mother's nightgown. One figure was almost bent, the other almost erect; one looked down at her feet, the other at a point forward. Two forms, almost an apparition, of the same soil, the same strength, the same faith. They walked together to the kitchen, slow, shuffling, pondering, irresolutely forward. The slippers shushed across the cold linoleum. My eyes hurt from the salt. I saw them walk together, intimate, close . . . as I would see them walk for all the years since.

"Come, Conrad. Have a bit of hot tea."

I saw her cry once. Basic training ended for all of us at Lackland Air Force Base in San Antonio. I had thirty days of furlough before they'd ship me overseas. We never mentioned it, but we all assumed that my destination would be Korea. If I had known, my orders indicated in semi-clear abbreviated language that my theater of operation was to be Alaska, but I never thought to decipher the white order papers that stayed on the bureau during my home stay.

It was time to catch my plane. Uncle Edmund waited in the car to drive me out to Logan Airport. I stood at the door with the heavy, untailored Air Force blues draped around me. Her face was serenely beautiful.

"Good-bye, Mom."

She leaned against me, my muscles young and strong, supporting her encircling arms. I kissed her on the cheek and it was wet. When I pulled away I saw the tears stream across the soft flesh. I knew she loved me. I knew now more than ever that she loved me. I never saw her cry before.

84

"I'll betcha five straight up."

"no man."

"I'll betcha five straight down then."

"no no man."

"Damn. Betcha can't make the fox with the gams."

"you ON! man you ON!"

EDMUND

Back in the twenties my Uncle Edmund was a great dancer, so they called him Jazz. It was a name that my grandmother disliked, so in respect for her wishes it was shortened to Jay. She didn't particularly like that either, but at least for all concerned it was an acceptable compromise. Grandmother and Ruby were sticklers for calling names properly. It was natural at times for one of Ruby's friends to refer to her as Rube. She would immediately correct the offender and punctuate the lesson with a cold stare. My friends chose to call me Connie, and for my family there was no nickname more despised. No one dared say the name in Mom's or Ruby's presence, so icy was the punishment they received. When I began receiving publicity as a high school track star, newsmen would refer to me only as Connie, and Mom and Ruby finally conceded to that greater force.

Edmund was my favorite person. I knew him through

the years as the whirling center of attention wherever he held court. He liked to dress in expensive and tasteful attire. Dress shirts were monogrammed, cuff links initialed, suits conservative and tailored, ties worn once and cashmere worn often. When he was present, people laughed and wanted to be near and tell their friends that they knew him. He had a gravelly voice that pushed out from behind flashing white teeth, and between the smile and the funny stories you were reduced to spasms of laughter and tears. Once he stood on the kitchen table and did an imitation of a Chinese running for mayor of Boston. My grandmother was so convulsed with laughter that she left the room in mirthful pain.

On warm weekends we'd motor to Cape Cod or Gloucester. Edmund always sported a new Olds or Buick and it was always black. Any other color was considered garish and outlandish. Those rides were the happiest days of my childhood. Edmund never spoke while driving. His steady concentration to wheel and highway was a calming influence on me in the back seat next to an aunt and a grandmother. The New England scenery passing by, with its rich greens and quiet wooden homes and harsh coastline, belonged to my uncle; through him this beauty and serenity were mine to inherit.

Each year we'd spend a few summer days at Martha's Vineyard. The "best" food was at the Vineyard. The "best" sunrises were at the Vineyard. I even got the "best" haircut ever at Martha's Vineyard. The island retreat was a pleasant ferry trip offshore from the Cape and close to fabled Nantucket Island. The villages and clay cliffs and miles of sandy beaches were a child's delight. I relished the scenic harbors that sheltered toylike sailboats with their masts like lollipop sticks standing at attention.

One summer, Edmund brought to the island an inflatable swimming suit. It was guaranteed to keep a non-swimming, pudgy-bellied, unathletic weekender afloat and on top of things in the great, green Atlantic. Edmund, following instructions, blew air through the rubber tube and into the air sacs, tied off the end and tucked it safely beneath his waistband, waded out into the gentle rises of salt water, eased onto his back, and delivered himself completely to American ingenuity. Moments later the round belly, brown toes, and relaxed head sank slowly from view, and like Atlantis would have been deposited to a subterranean resting place if the descent had not been interrupted by a sputtering and angry emergence from wet ocean to dry beach. Edmund never went in the water again.

He married twice but had no children. Some of his friends believed I was his son; others thought I was his brother. Once Ruby told me that Edmund would be by the house later to see me. He had a bet with some people that I was really his son, and I was to answer accordingly. Later Edmund pulled up in a car and waited for me to run over to say hello. There were several others in the car.

"Tell 'em who you are, Conrad."

"I'm Conrad Balfour."

"Yah. Thas' right. But tell 'em who I am. Who am I, now?"

"You're Uncle Edmund."

His face became hard. The others laughed. I knew he wanted me to call him Dad. Something within me wouldn't allow that. I never learned what that was all about, and the years went by with all of them dying, and my queries iced away into stillness.

I was his favorite person, too. There was nothing he wouldn't do for me, and I knew this. If anything had happened to him, it would have shattered my world. It almost happened once in New York. Grandmother called me to her chair and said, "Don't cry now, but Uncle George has had an accident. He was stabbed in New York City."

I didn't cry. I was scared and afraid to inquire further, but I didn't cry. Later that day my grandmother said there was a mistake — it was Edmund who had been stabbed. My mind exploded in confusion and torment enveloped me. The tears broke like floodwater and my loud bawling finally evoked a stern rebuke from Mom to get hold of myself. Edmund pulled through, but I felt disquieting waves of guilt that Edmund was more important to me than was George.

Like all the family, Edmund was a mystery. I knew that he worked in the Boston underworld, that he ran the numbers game in at least the South End, and that his 411 Bar was a hangout for the sordid and sainted. As a kid I was never allowed in there, but as I grew older the rules were relaxed to the point where I could enter, exchange greetings, and sit in a booth for no longer than a few minutes. Bartenders treated me with a friendliness reserved for special citizens. Sometimes I'd see customers looking my way and perhaps whispering, "That's Jay's boy. Don't they look alike?" Police would walk in with the daily paper stuck under their arms and laugh with Edmund. Plainclothes detectives drank scotch there. Handsome, tough Syrians, Italians, and Armenians flashed in with their colored shirts and blond women. Lawyers with baggy pants and food droppings on their ties sat next to leather briefcases, while black prostitutes perched crosslegged at the bar with yellow liquid in white glasses and cigarettes that were hot orange at one end and sticky red at the other.

Ruby said that if a girl ever approached me, Edmund would run her out of town. His protectiveness of me never seemed suffocating, but it was so all-encompassing that either I never knew it was in operation or else I didn't admit to it. Street gangs roamed the area, but never the South End. We were exempt from all outside forces that might intrude on our harmony and territorial peace.

When I was nine years old, twice weekly I'd walk to choir practice at the Cathedral of the Holy Cross. The church was in a tough neighborhood run by the Collins brothers. One night thirty of us were lined up against the cathedral wall by Tommy and Franny Collins and robbed of all possessions — marbles, waxed baseball cards, change, jackknives. Tommy later was to gain fame as the second-ranked lightweight fighter in the world, who on title night was decked eight times by reigning champ Jimmy Carter. As the brothers moved down the line, robbing each tenor, soprano, and alto, they came to me and Franny said, "Beat it, kid — you're Jazz's boy."

Alice Pennington (this isn't her real name) knew that I was bashful near girls. I might have been sixteen then and she three or four years older, pretty, blond, and popular. Some of us were standing on a street corner when Alice came up behind me and threw her arms about my chest. I could feel her body against my buttocks . . . the warm sensation was delicious. The guys laughed and Alice held on tighter. When she finally released me I was sure that sex was beautiful. The following day I heard that Alice was beaten roughly by her boyfriend, M.M., a small-time hood who ran a South End pool hall. He was teaching her a lesson regarding body contact with young black kids.

A few days went by and M.M. was found on the tracks

under a freight train. Both his legs were crushed and had to be amputated. The family code for those embracing the rackets was so far-reaching and out of perspective that a man lost half of his body because he had beaten a girl for flirting with an untouchable boy.

All the years I loved Edmund, I never heard him express a gut feeling or talk of love and hate or share family experiences or discuss his friends. He came close once. Brinks headquarters was robbed in Boston. It was a sensational crime that made worldwide news. With uncharacteristic candor I asked him about it. He must have been surprised, but he looked past me and softly answered, "They used to bring food to Mom when you lived at 78 Middlesex. Specs gave you candy and those balls you used to play with. I hope they never lay a finger on 'em." (Specs O'Keefe, one of the robbers, had owned a candy store next to the 411 Bar. He later turned state's evidence when his co-conspirators held out on his share of the money.)

Edmund was true to code, even to me. He lived by instinct and the wary knowledge of whom to trust, and that was nobody. The good times went only as far as the funny stories and the laughter and the picking up of the bill. One night he was struck by a car on Tremont Street. When people flocked around his fallen body, Edmund pulled out a huge roll of money from his pants. "Hold this," he said to a curious onlooker. "I don't want the fluff to get it."

Once his wife told me that Jay always mocked disdainfully those crooks who, when arrested, covered their faces with their wide hats. "Whad's with them? They go into Stetson and say, 'Hey, give me a hat . . . real expensive . . . the best. I wanna go first cabin when they bust me, then I kin cover up my pretty face.' Whad's with them? They got their names plastered all over the city and they hidin' their faces!!''

But Edmund had never been busted himself. Then one month the 411 was staked out by the FBI. They were more interested in Edmund's boss, a Mafia lord, than in Edmund. The news media must have been tipped off, because on the day of the raid the cameras were all there. Under the 411 in a soundproof numbers room, Edmund and friends were totaling receipts. When the feds broke in upstairs, a buzzer rasped in the numbers room and alerted the men that there was trouble. Columbus Avenue had a series of tunnels leading away from the 411 and out under almost any brownstone up the street. The men were sent away through these while Edmund remained behind to destroy paper evidence. Then he followed the men out of the basement, through the tunnels, and into a tenement flat many doors away. Afterwards he walked up the street and into the 411 as if nothing had happened. The feds immediately grabbed him and hurried him to a black security car outside. When he reached the avenue teeming with spectators, cameras, and reporters, Uncle Edmund had his hat in his hand covering up his face.

Edmund never recovered from that experience. It wasn't that he did time or was bodily mishandled by police. He wasn't. Some of the police were his friends. It just seemed to take it all out of him. The laughs were less spontaneous. The walk was slower. The paunchy stomach got even softer and his weight went up. The enthusiasm for late meals in Syrian restaurants with lots of loud company gave way to eating quietly with only a few companions.

By this time I was married and lived with my family in the Midwest. When we visited Boston, Edmund's old enthusiasm revved up. He would spark when my small daughter Sharon was mentioned. It was with Sharon, the firstborn, the daughter he never had, as it had been with me . . . the son who wasn't his. He loved her big. Very big. She perpetuated the hope in his loins.

He called Sharon's name from under the oxygen tent in Boston's Floating Hospital. When Sharon, then age eight, and I reached his bedside, he was already in the arms of death. His liver was atrophied from long hours immersed in Schenley's and Canadian Club, his face puffy and yellowed. I whispered to him that we had come, but he never answered. She loved him, but he passed on not knowing she was there, his body a rattling chamber of secrets and silences.

They fired twenty-one guns at his funeral. The gangsters were there with their women, and his family, and his Turkish father's children, grandchildren, and great-grandchildren, and the hangers-on and the suckers and the fluff. They were all there. Most of them called me his son. Or his brother. None of them knew who I really was. But at that they probably knew me better than they did him.

It was a goddamn sad funeral.

Once she was a little girl
tum, tum
And then she grew.
Then she had a little boy.
tum
Who never knew.

Boy grew - asked who?

She told him when he was a man
tum, tum
And then he knew.

RUBY

I never see her as a child. Grandmother — I see *her* as a child, with skinny legs under a cotton dress, small and frisky. But not Ruby. Now that it's mostly in the past — the visits to Boston, the lengthy letters, the exchange of gifts, the funeral — I see her yet. Ill and guilt-laden, lonely, self-doubting, afraid — she was the single most remarkable person who ever entered my world. The packet of her letters before me, a small brown address book, the sepia snapshot from her citizenship papers, two locks of soft hair she saved from my second year of life . . . they are softly sad. Through misted eyelids she appears this wintry day, each of my pauses recalling the mosaics that laid out our past. I see her with coat snugged about her shoulders in Boston's wet winters. I see her with summer frock before the desk writing a note to the florist. I see her touch wine with rich lips, or setting the dining table with accurate etiquette. Mostly I see her reading the current bestseller, her leather monogrammed bookmark temporarily jutting from an unread page. But never do I see her as a child. Only as Ruby. Aunt Ruby. Ruby Agatha Beckair, the beautiful daughter of Rosella, who, at age eighteen, gave me birth, and for nearly a half century thereafter, suffered a life of tortured denial.

Her face would have been revered in Damascus or Persia. The oriental head was warm and delicate. Fragility rested at the cheekbones, about the almond eyes, across the soft chin. Even the energy in her lips, the firmness of her nose, and the vitality of her brows were kept in repose by her elegance. The combination was fascinating. Her tiny waist — she weighed just a hundred pounds — joined clear lines of thighs to the gentle upward swing of grace supporting her beautiful face.

She was so proud of me. Every morning she would take an ivory brush and stroke my hair until it bristled with electric charge. We'd take short walks and people would stop to admire and beam. Sometimes I'd keep up with Ruby in a red pedal car with real rubber tires and electric lights and my initials in gold scroll. Ruby said that one Christmas I was dying with fever, so she and my grandmother let me have the car early. It had cost one hundred dollars. They believed the present helped me get through, and now when I moved along Middlesex Street, cars stopped to let me have my regal right of way.

Children in the neighborhood attended each of my birthday parties like snobbish Greek Houses at Harvard across the Charles. I remember liking tiny Yvonne, but when she came to the door, Ruby told her she wasn't invited. It was a cruelty never forgotten.

Once I ran away. Or at least I thought I had. I went around the block to Emerald Street, knowing that only God could find one so far from home. But suddenly there was Ruby . . . my lord, is this world so small . . . clutching my hand and pulling me toward that brownstone in the other world. There was company at the house, but Ruby never put off a punishment. Uncle George's shaving strap, slit in four tails at one end, was taken down from its resting place behind the iron stove. I was made to strip naked and receive a whipping on my bare haunches. The greatest pain was having our company see me punished. I never ran from home again.

Growing up was a series of disciplines, harshly and effectively applied:

"DON'T talk back to your elders!"

"How DARE you interrupt while I'm talking!"

"I DIDN'T hear anyone say please, now did I?"

"To bed! Immediately!"

"Wipe your mouth with the NAPKIN. You are a gentleman."

We moved to a new neighborhood when I was thirteen. 200 West Springfield Street was still the South End, but our neighbors were mostly black now. Sometimes, in the alley behind our house, men would ask me if I wanted to spend a little time with them. I never knew what they meant, but I knew enough to say "no" — or rather, "no thank you." Ruby's discipline was branded on me. I wanted to ask her what those men wanted, but it was impossible to ask questions in a home that never answered them.

One evening after a Boy Scout meeting, Whitey Wanionek and I walked to the Boston Commons to hear Jack Benny's Rochester hawk war bonds. There was a large crowd. An Italian was standing in front of me with his hands resting behind him. Soon I felt his fingers playing across my pants fly. I was confused and moved away.

Whitey slid into my spot. Moments later Whitey hit the man across the head and we both ran like bandits across the Commons to Tremont Street. "That bastard was a fag!" Whitey panted.

When I was seventeen years old, Ruby talked to me once about "sometimes when you're with a girl things could be difficult . . . it might be wise to use a rubber." That was all. I was embarrassed. I had never kissed a girl in my life, never touched a girl. Oh yes, Violet had kissed me in the basement at Middlesex Street when I was nine. And when I was eleven Anna across the street shook her breasts at me. But rubbers were so ugly. Guys had them in wallets, wrinkled and gray and contorted like gargoyle faces.

Ruby had a way of extorting the purest moral conduct from me, simply by describing my father. "He was a gentleman. A genuine bred gentleman. So courteous. So kind. He would be proud of you, Conrad. You are so like him. He would be proud."

As she talked, I'd picture a tall, thin man with coffee skin, wearing a tan cashmere topcoat and looking down on me in front of the house on Middlesex. His hands were on my shoulders and as I looked up at him we smiled. The vague image was a deliciously warm blanket that wrapped Ruby's words and my picture together into one. He looked kind. He acted courteous. I wanted to be like him. Have him be proud of me.

Ruby and I would look at each other. Silently. Who is my father? I didn't ask. Who is my mom? Was she your sister? Why don't you tell me if she was kind? If she was courteous? Why don't you tell me? God no! Don't tell me anything. Maybe it's bad! We looked at each other in silence. It was often like this . . . looking into each other's brown eyes in some sort of silent roar.

I spent a year in Des Moines, Iowa, attending Drake University. Ruby was visiting a friend in Los Angeles and wanted to stop off at the campus on her return to Boston. "I won't embarrass you. If you think people will guess that you're colored, I can be introduced as a friend of your family."

"Hell, Ruby. They know I'm Negro. I can't even live on campus. Negroes live *off* campus. Don't worry about it."

She rode the train to Des Moines and we spent almost a day together. I showed her my room and introduced her to my roommate. He flipped over her and flirted outrageously. Soon he had the whole street prancing up to our room to meet this "solid 'A' fox."

That evening we walked to town for pizza. We sat in the restaurant for an embarrassing minute after minute, no one serving us, no one even approaching our table to ask us to leave. We looked at each other, too proud to admit that we were being slighted.

"I guess we'd better go, Ruby."

"If you wish, dear."

Her letters were masterpieces. She selected stationery that matched the wisdom of her words. On one, a brown pastel sheet, her typed message began:

My dear, dear Conrad:

While walking with a friend through the back streets of Florence, Michelangelo noticed a block of marble half buried in dirt, rubble, and mire; he lifted it to the surprise of his friend, who asked what he saw in such a worthless piece of rock.

"Oh, there's an angel in that stone and I must bring it out," was Michelangelo's famous reply. As you know, he brought the marble to his studio and worked patiently and lovingly on it until he brought out the hidden glory that was to inspire others.

The point is, God Himself put His own image in every human being. You, too, are God's instrument, bringing out what is true, good, and beautiful even in the worst of men.

When her mother died, she wrote:

Forget? When it pours rain her dear face is at the window watching for me. When it's cold her kind voice says "bundle up." When I can't unzipper my dress, where are those gentle hands that complete my toilet . . . when the radio is loud a tender voice says "turn it down" . . . when it's dark a laughing voice says "Ruby, aren't you asleep yet?" And I go on and on. Every corner, every breath I draw, every wind that sighs, brings her home to me. But she left . . . without gaining consciousness . . . without a smile . . . she just left me. She was the only one who said "Ruby" like the sound of music . . . .

Sometimes she would write in longhand, the calligraphy stroked in bold and flaring trails of slender ink. Her letter i's were never dotted but wreathed in halos, and for years I found myself circling that vowel in the same manner.

Our house had numerous pictures of Christ and it seemed there was a rosary in every bureau drawer. I was raised a Catholic although the rest of the family was Protestant. Ruby converted to Catholicism until I became an adult and moved away from home. Then she went back to her former Protestantism.

When I joined the United States Air Force, my grandmother and Ruby were living in Roxbury. By the time I was discharged, four years later, they had moved to Brockton, a suburb just south of Boston. Coming home on military leave, I was struck by the number of pictures of me in each room. Their bedroom had a snapshot of me wearing a letter jacket from high school. On the wall, I was reclining on the grass in Des Moines. In the hall a giant blowup in dress uniform. In the living room Edmund and I were in bathing suits. In the den a sketch of me by Collette Ashenbach, a German artist. The house looked like a scrapbook!

After my years in the Air Force, I married and moved to North Dakota. I worked as a radio announcer for a time, then sold enrollments for Dale Carnegie courses. I traveled across the state, weeks at a crack, until I had one or more classes put together. It was sometimes a lonely existence on the Dakota prairies, but I loved the farmers and their church-going wives who wondered at a man who didn't drink coffee. I loved the desolate, flat land and the ghost-fog of snow floating across the roads in a dreamy tumbleweed of mist.

My wife Rose and I were unhappy with the travel and our marriage was deteriorating. I would work until close to midnight, then cuddle in a motel bed with magazines and books until I fell asleep with the lamp full on. Sometimes I'd have a radio, and I'd listen to distant stations wander in and fade out. I'd think of my parents and wonder who they were. For some reason, here on the prairie, it started to bother me more than before. My heart was always heavy. I'd head for my room at day's end, strip myself of clothes, and shower. While the spigot rained on me, I'd cry. I knew that not even God could see my tears here. Rose sensed my despair. She'd sometimes ask why I didn't ask Ruby who my parents were, but I never responded.

I don't recall the town, but at noon one day there was a message for me from Rose.

"What's up?"

"One of your parents is still living."

"What!?" I was stunned. "Who?"

"Your mother."

"Well, who is she?"

"It's Ruby . . . "

"Ruby?! *Ruby* is my mother?!"

"Myself, I always thought so. I told her you were bothered. She's afraid you won't love her."

"Of course, I . . . I love her. I do."

"She says your dad died at sea. He was Welsh."

I didn't know what to do with myself. My God, I never even suspected. How could I have been so blind? I was thirty-three years old — I had lived with her for twenty-five years — and I knew her only as my aunt. Did Ruby think now she could save my marriage by admitting to being my mother?

Soon a letter arrived. She begged me to think of my children, urged me not to worry about my background, and then told me about my father:

Your father was white, 27 years old. If he did not predecease his older brother his title would have been "Sir." He was a wonderful guy. Very considerate, average looking with the straightest nose you ever saw, dark complexion with dark brown hair — not a wave in it. 5 feet 9 inches, and 145 pounds. To see him was to *know* he was good — never heard an unkind word of him or from him about anyone. Very quiet-spoken — never heard him raise his voice. An English gentleman to his fingertips.

I knew him for a glorious year. I was 18 and couldn't make up my mind to leave for England with him, and I was afraid to leave Mom and wanted time to think. Then he had to leave for 3 months. The night before he left — the inevitable. He didn't even know, he didn't even know I was pregnant. That's what makes this whole thing horrible even now.

Excuse me, dear, this is the first time I've again faced it (other than infrequently Mom would say "When are you going to tell Conrad?") and I find I'm in tears.

I carried tiny — from 100 pounds to 112. I didn't know for four months. Edmund never knew — he was married and hardly visited. George *may* have suspected. Neighbors didn't know — Mom sent me to Rhode Island. When you were born she brought you home and I remained to recuperate.

I was heartbroken and shocked — I tried to destroy myself twice but Mom prevented it. Watched me like an eagle. During the last months I lost touch with reality. I was a very sick girl — but for Mom neither of us would be here now.

Darling, is this a mistake — should I wish both of us were destroyed years ago? Happiness has eluded me — but when I watch you, hear your voice or hear of you, see the goodness in you — this is happiness.

Just before you and Rose came home — getting my room ready for both of you, I took his pack of letters and destroyed them along with the letter from the government telling me he had died. When I didn't hear as usual, I wrote. He never knew, never knew. Name: Garth Robert Balfour.

I sincerely hope you can forgive me. I haven't any excuse to offer in self defense. And although I ask it I don't expect forgiveness for the heartaches I must have caused you, for you see, I haven't quite forgiven myself yet. I undoubtedly have estranged you — it will take time for you to become accustomed to my feet of clay, I'll go along with that. But please dear, don't you have feet of clay. By that I mean, do not let my mistake embitter you. I've had a lifelong regret bottled in me. It was not easy to write something never voiced — I wouldn't have done it now if I didn't consider it urgent.

I know I've failed you bitterly. Many times over the years I have thought of a thing or two and winced, realizing how I've failed you. I can't think of a single outstanding act of mine towards you. You must have been terribly lonesome growing up . . . . To say I love you is so trite, for love is actions, not words. I am unworthy of you — I shirked my responsibility and left it all to Mom and now I'm thoroughly ashamed.

Oh, I brought you up as a Catholic because Garth would have liked it. God love, I do.

Ruby

After that, I visited Brockton yearly. We somehow never resumed opening up the early years. She once referred to the packet of letters bound with a red ribbon that always rested on the bureau in the room she prepared for me. "I knew you would never pry. I never feared your discovering them. They were his letters, but I had to destroy them . . . finally."

Rose and I were living in Minneapolis now. To our three children Aunt Ruby was a faraway Santa who always sent books and funny cards and little purses filled with coins. When they learned she was coming to visit, they could hardly restrain themselves. What room would she stay in . . . would she bring her French poodle . . . what food did she like? Ruby had asked me not to reveal to the children that she was my mother. She was still full of guilt and vanity and could not bear to think of anyone knowing her secret.

It was early 1971. Ruby and her poodle Pierre lived alone in the house in Brockton. She worked for the commonwealth as a social worker. She'd been having headaches and at their worst was forced to take time away from her job. Days passed and no word. One of her co-workers called Uncle George expressing concern. He and his wife Lorraine drove out to the house and found Ruby in darkness. She was incoherent at first and didn't recognize them. At Massachusetts General Hospital, they discovered a malignant tumor on her brain. She was operated on immediately, then given six months to a year to live.

I saw her following her surgery. Her head was bound heavily with bandages and her eyes were blackened. Both of us were happy, though, for the opportunity to visit. She said the pain was great.

"George and Lorraine are taking care of Pierre. He's about as cute as you." She laughed. "I have my books, but it's too much. Can't read or watch TV." Then suddenly, "Conrad, do you know if I'm going to die?"

I was able to arrange for her to spend her last days in Minnesota with me. I lived alone; by this time my marriage was over. So I selected an apartment on Lake Calhoun for Ruby and myself. My hope was that she'd live out the spring and enjoy walks amidst squirrels, robins, and bicycles.

Each day we'd walk by the lake. I'd bundle her in scarf and boots and describe how pretty the lake would be in spring. Ruby looked full into my face when I talked, but as the days passed she was able to walk less often, and soon, too, her speech faded away.

Her mind was rapidly deteriorating and retreating to childish meanderings. She'd go into disjointed sentences like those of a child struggling with new sounds. We could never communicate verbally anymore, except to say "I love you." For me it was a rebirth, knowing a mother.

Outside, it was cold — below twenty degrees. The lake was mothwhite and the snow had settled in for a long stay, but it was a summer sky. Clouds puffed softly above and the sky broke around them in a wide umbrella. I entered the apartment and saw Ruby huddled in a corner of the couch. She had covered herself with an Indian blanket, and her eyes stared out into the stillness of the room.

"Hiiiiy." She prolonged the word. The vowels came out covered with wool.

"You okay? How are you?"

She stared. Then she reached out her arms to me. I held her and snuggled my head into her purple robe. Out of the semi-darkness came: "Diiie. Diiie."

My face turned up to her. She wore the expression of a child. "Diiie. Diiie."

"Yes, Mom." We looked full into each other. I whispered, "Yes. Yes."

There were no sounds. Then there *were* sounds. I felt the tears building inside my face and the shudders like distant thunder beginning to threaten. I pulled away, went to the bedroom, and lost myself in tears.

She died in February, 1972. I had hoped she would make it until spring.

three

it's a long ride back

to suckle that breast . . .

but leavin' that teat

is the ride I luvs best

1971

Late one January night, I dropped in at the Minneapolis Jewish Community Center and listened to a lecture on crime. I was late and only got the last few minutes of the program. When the meeting broke up I said a few goodnights and drove out on Highway 12. A right turn took me to beautiful Cedar Lake Boulevard, which hugs and caresses the lake for about a half mile. One stop sign held me up before I could take that restful ride and then go to bed. Something slammed into the door on my side. I knew what it was immediately. The car shot ahead and didn't stop until I pulled up before my apartment building. I got out and looked at the door. Clean and round and small and neat was the empty eye of a bullet hole. I stuck my little finger into it, walked into the house, and did some long thinking in the warmth of my bed.

Cheri-Pat Dale was a member of the growing legion of honest people. There was no room in her style of life for games, hypocrisy, or hatred. She had just shared with me a warm segment of a day in her life when long ago and far away she spent some time in Manhattan. I liked her immensely.

I was in Bozeman, Montana, for a speaking engagement, and Cheri-Pat and her family had done everything possible to make my visit comfortable. One day they decided to drive over to Yellowstone and show me all its wonders. At Old Faithful, Cheri-Pat and I walked a mile or so through trails and rugged rock formations. We talked of politics and race and ecology and love. But Cheri-Pat talked of love in a very special way. Better than most anybody. She froze the moment and passed it from her lips to my heart to carry and share.

"I was in New York on one of those crowded subways. You know how they push and dig in. Without my will I was driven to an overhead strap and just held on, driving the balls of my feet into the floor. Then I noticed this lady. She was sitting right in front of me. An old lady. She had her hands in her lap. Just resting. Her hands were beautiful . . . so beautiful and long and skinny with blue veins pressing up to the white ceiling of her skin. I fell in love with them . . . so delicate . . . so old. I forgot that I could fall and I lowered both my hands to her lap and clasped those long fingers in my hands. She looked up, into my face, and we smiled. When the train stopped, both of us got off and I asked her if she wanted to share a Coke. She shook her head and smiled again. 'I'd like a frankfurter and an orange drink.' We ate and giggled and crumpled napkins and then hugged good-bye."

Cheri-Pat pursed her lips and looked up at my face. "Do you like that story?"

He was the most imposing figure of them all. His face and carriage and air of mystery could well have found comfort in any age. He could have walked the sands of Treasure Island or the sea-washed deck of the *Bounty*. The body was thick and strong, the hands partly gnarled and wide. Like all his brothers, he walked high and majestically. He walked as if the earth were a billiard-smooth ball and its only projection the six-foot brown of his frame.

This was enough. This was all Clyde Bellecourt needed to stand above a crowd, to match his charisma against the electric of other fascinating figures. Yet there was more. He had a voice. A voice immodestly magnificent. A voice never wasted. A group would talk of governors and issues and small solutions with courteous interruptions and quick enthusiasm while Clyde kept the thunder quiet in his gut. It was like a cat, waiting to pounce up and out until ready to leap back into the cave from whence it came. The sound made you recall thick Maracaibo coffee and fresh surgarcane, coconut meat, and mud. It was burnished steel and mixing cement . . . the door to a metal vault or a black sky.

We were on our return trip from a town out West where we had spent two days speaking to groups from the Jaycees' state convention. We weren't quite sure that they had appreciated either one of us. The plane miled through the cold late night. All of the cabin was in darkness except for the light above the seat between us. My waist ached and my feet were tired; most of the trip was a bummer and my mind wanted out. Midnight was on my wrist and the rest my eyes pleaded for was being granted. Until . . . the voice. It was almost a command to come alert. Up it droned. Out it came.

"My wife is tired of all this. The traveling. The loneliness. And you know? I am too."

That was all. He was finished. It was his greatest confession. It stunned me. This warrior must know that his wife will never see that day. I closed my eyes and cursed the fate that I knew would lay him down to sleep before his time.

It might have been 9 P.M. The meeting had been called for an hour earlier. I'd been in this storefront office many times. The American Indian Movement had its headquarters in this old room. I'd been here when the director and female lead of the movie "A Man Called Horse" had come to defend the picture. I'd played rummy here. Been given beads and a leather vest here. Even slept overnight here. I was here again for a meeting about which I actually knew little. A call had come to me from Dennis Banks in Miami. He and his friend Clyde Bellecourt had had a dispute. One was president of AIM, the other its director. I assumed the meeting was to patch things up again.

There were only eight or nine people in the room. I was surprised at the small number; surely this meeting was important enough to attract a larger audience. Dennis was on the phone and waved when he saw me. His black hair fell below his shoulders and the black headband forced my eyes to zero in on his strong chestnut face. George Mitchell was with him, another Chippewa. George was always friendly, and we talked for a moment or more.

Some chairs were carried in from the back and put in classroom order up front, facing a table. Dennis announced that things should begin.

"Can we sit up here so we can start the session?"

No one moved. Five minutes went by and Dennis looked at his notes.

"Can we sit up here? It's kind of tough on the voice to talk to the back of the room."

Two women moved to chairs in the second row. A burly man moved to the side. Another to the center. The rest stayed in the rear — one with a baby, another with a small child. Dennis sat at the table and let another five minutes crawl by. It was an excruciating test of patience. I suddenly sensed the hostility directed against Dennis. The uneasiness in the room. Dennis, who had grown to a man here, started the movement here, drank, counseled, and built tactics here, was no longer among friends. I felt that the night would be historic.

"Judy. Would you keep minutes? Might have a libel suit and someone would want the record." He laughed.

Judy said, "Why don't you ask Marcel?"

"If I ask Marcel she'll say to ask you. Do we have a tape recorder?"

No one moved. Mitchell was now at the table sitting with Dennis. At least three minutes elapsed before another word was spoken. Then Dennis said, "I'd like to explain what our position is. But first let's hear from George."

George Mitchell waited three minutes before speaking. It was amazing. The periods of silence were unprecedented in my experience. George spoke for only a minute or two and turned the meeting back to Dennis. For the next hour I was spellbound. Dennis stood and paced, pausing frequently . . . his voice rarely rising . . . his manner subtle as sand . . . his message blunt as a blowtorch.

I have to go back a long way. I have no motive other than to show all of you that I care for our people. I'm sorry that Clyde is not here but I know that he cares for our people just as much. They must have thought me stubborn a few years ago — Clyde, his brother Vernon, Russell Means. All of them were pushing for an addition to our constitution. You've heard of Article

310. We all have. It said that any officer of AIM involved in drinking to excess while on duty would be subject to dismissal. I was against Article 310. I'd been drinking for years and I fought their proposal. You know me. I drank every day. Every day! I argued with Vernon, I argued with Clyde, I argued with everybody. But they insisted and they won out. So Article 310 became part of the AIM constitution.

One day in this office the phone rang. That phone right over there. It was an Indian from Fort Totten saying that one of our people was in jail and could we help them. Well, we couldn't send anybody. He calls again and pleads for help. I remember Frank in Fargo and promised that I'll try to get him over to Totten. I call Frank and Frank comes to the phone. I ask him if he would drive up to Fort Totten and he says he'll leave right away. He says it'll take him about five hours.

I call Fort Totten back and tell them that Frank will be there in six hours. Seven hours later, Fort Totten calls and wants to know where our man is. I call Fargo and Frank answers the phone again. He's at a party and he sounds drunk. For the second time he promises to leave immediately. I call Totten again and tell them Frank is on his way. The next morning comes and Totten calls and says that AIM hasn't shown yet. Do you think I'm embarrassed? I call Frank and he's still in that damn party. This time I tell him to order everyone out of the room and when he does I'll hang up. He tells his friends to get out of there and as far as I can tell he seems to be finally on his way to Fort Totten.

By this time I'm ready to board my plane to Omaha.

When I register in an Omaha hotel there are messages from my office. From my wife. And from Fort Totten. When I get the call through I'm told that my man has arrived but he's drunk. I'm told to get him out of town, that they don't want him, that he's to stay away from the jailhouse, and that AIM can go to hell. Before I can reach Frank, Fort Totten reaches me one last time. Frank had gained admittance to the jailed Indian after all. When Frank left him, the man — who had only one arm — hanged himself in his cell.

I was so angry that I called the national AIM office and got Jerry to leave his home and go to the office, get out the constitution, mail a copy of Article 310 to every director in the country, and send a letter to Frank telling him he was fired! I wasn't angry at the directors. I felt we were all as guilty as Frank because we had all abused the rule. We had it but we never enforced it. I myself was drunk as often as anybody. But Frank broke my back. When he left Fort Totten he was off to take his kids out on an Easter hunt. Hell, that's a ritual that's not even Indian! Since that day I've quit drinking. I also tried to get a meeting with the directors to discuss Article 310, but they wouldn't listen. They fought to get it in but they wouldn't back up my action on a man who abused it. Sure, I know. I didn't have any power to fire Frank, but I was angry and reacting. The important point is that no one wants to do anything about the problem. And the problem is drinking on duty.

At Cass Lake we tried to show our power against merchants and residents who have abused Indians for years. Our people came from all over the country. We had a strategy. We were going to blockade the tourist trade. Right? We had the merchants right where we wanted them. Some of us were ready to give up our lives. Drinking was strictly forbidden. Our sentries had loaded rifles and we were calling for a show-down. So what happens? Liquor! If firing had broken out we would have hit more of our own people than the opposition. The blockade was a flop. I saw more clearly than ever that Article 310 was absolutely needed.

I appreciate your patience. Let me tell you about Rapid City. We were the first Indian organization to get into that disaster area and help the situation. Whites and Indians are together. Everyone is helping. Everyone is pulling together. AIM gets access to manpower, a helicopter, combines, and shovels. When the flood lets up a bit I'm asked to speak to a large group of the citizens. I tell them that we're proud to work side by side with all the residents . . . we're proud to be here. Before I can complete my speech one of the national AIM leaders staggers up to the stage and wrestles the mike from me. He shouts, "Who do you think you are? I'll do the talking around here! Get the hell out of here!" He's so drunk he can hardly speak clearly. I storm off that stage holding down my rage as best I can. I'll tell you all right now: In Washington, D.C., they respect us. We can appear before the legislature and they know we'll be there on time. If it's seven in the morning we'll be there. If it's seven at night we'll be there then. In Rapid City? In Rapid City they think we're full of shit!

Another time a meeting is just about breaking up. As I walk past one of our cars filled with Indians I smell the stench of pot. I've been on that stuff as much as any of you. Pot and whiskey. But now I see it as a poison. I hit the side of that car with my fist, and I tell them they should be shot by a firing squad.

Or what about the Democratic National Convention? We're just about to drive down to Miami when we get a call from a town in Arizona that seven of our people are busted. A vote is taken and we decide to drive down there to help out. I call our Washington attorney and then we start down with ten packed cars. By the time we pull in to that town there are only two cars. Mine and Clyde's. No one else shows. Where the hell did they go? Our attorney had flown in and beat us by hours. The sheriff is really an all-right guy. All of our busted victims were arrested for their own protection. They were stoned! If they go to trial they'll throw away the key. All the sheriff was doing was letting them sleep it off.

We've got to start caring. I'm on the wagon. I'm not saying we should give up drinking. I'm saying that on duty — during a protest or a demonstration — we can't afford to blow it with stupid actions.

I'm finished with my explanation.

A baby started to cry. No one tried to hush the disturbance. To this group, family sounds were never disturbances. A deep male voice said, "I don't appreciate your telling me when I can or can't drink."

George Mitchell moved in with, "We're not saying that. David in Milwaukee can stay on the wagon for at least five days. He doesn't let drinking get in the way of business."

A female responded: "I think you reacted too soon, Dennis. I wish that you and Clyde could get together."

Another: "You didn't have the power to fire Frank. It was up to the local AIM head, not a national officer."

A male: "I have to admit that I was unhappy with receiving that copy of Article 310. I drink beer. Why should you send me that letter? The white man drinks just as much. Show me where he is willing to forego liquor at a business meeting."

A male: "You sound like the BIA." Dennis smiled at him. Inside he had to be wincing. To be compared to the Bureau of Indian Affairs was the supreme insult. "You come down here from your lofty perch in Washington and try to tell us how to run our lives. You want to help? You really want to help? Go back to your big office and meet with all those legislators that respect you. We've got AIM offices all over the country. Get us, each one of us, some money — get this AIM office $50,000. Then you'll be helping, baby!"

Dennis spoke softly. "I can't get you anything. I'm not your leader. You fired me in last month's meeting. Twenty-six cities have asked me to be their national director. This city is not one of them. If you want money, ask your leader."

A male: "I'm no hophead, Dennis. But don't tell me when to drink."

"All I'm asking you is: What are you going to do? Meetings, conciliations, shaking hands, articles and constitutions, power to dismiss . . . that's incidental now. What are you going to do? What are you going to do about the drinking, about the narcotics?"

No one said a word this time. A child could be heard in the back, shuffling across the floor. Mitchell and Banks were stonefaced, their eyes going past the chairs and onlookers to the rear of the room. Now nothing stirred. My thoughts weighed heavily in my head. The room grew heavy, too, with the burdening silence. You've heard of time seeming to stand still. Here the silence was screaming and we could not escape. The words "What are you going to do?" riveted us to our chairs.

Somewhere in time George said, "We are copyrighting the name AIM to make sure no one can abuse it again."

Dennis looked down. He spoke for the last time. "Tell your children they can aspire to the highest Indian office in the land. They can dream of being a director for the American Indian Movement. They can fill the position by being a dope pusher and a drunkard. I started AIM in this city. It makes me sad and heavy in my heart to be unwelcome here now. If you are ever in Washington my doors will always be open. You will be welcome."

His eyes caught mine and he nodded. My body was stiff. I got up and walked over to George and Dennis. George smiled and hugged me. Dennis put his hand in my belt and pulled me toward him.

"You're still in there, aren't you."

"Yah."

His face was older, sad and unsmiling and sallow. I looked up into his eyes and knew that he was a great man. A very great man.

When he's drowsy he nods.

Isn't that strange?

When he's saddened he sobs.

Isn't that strange?

Lights a butt with a match

Itchy skin makes him scratch

go-doddle-dee bagadee pritch-itee change

If that isn't oddly, peculiarly, strange.

JOE

You gettin' three a day. They're not squares, but hey, we got folks out there don't eat no way as good. But don't be thankful for the grub. They don't print no ads advertising it. Hey, don't be thankful. Regrets. Leavin' that woman and those kids. If you ain't regrettin' you forgettin'. We let 'em down. Bad. Hey, all of us. That's not cool."

Joe had a way of tailoring his delivery, his language. It depended on the audience. White urbanites were fed an easy diet of colloquialisms. Schoolchildren were given enough hip to honor their avowed separation from adults. This audience was prison peers. They were black, mostly. And he was their elected leader. Their Prime Minister. All the P.M.'s were eloquent. All were organizers. All were a safety buffer between the tenants of Sandstone Federal

Correctional Institution and the keepers. But only this
P.M. — Joseph Archie — inspired. Friday and Sunday
evenings, week after week, Joe stood before them and
inspired. Their sentence of time, inexorable, glacial,
paralytic, became in his hands chunks of rubble that they
could rebuild into castles of hope in a clearly foreseeable
tomorrow.

Part of it was the language and the wisdom. "You hatin'
whitey. Right? You a fool then. His high life expectancy
gets him a yard of years for blues and disease. Hate's a
raven, tappin', tappin'. If'n you don't open the window, no
way he build a nest in the kitchen."

Part of it was his manner and presence. Tall, thin, a good
dark blackness. His eyes moved slowly, assessing the electricity around his own center . . . the field of charge and
voltage his own creation.

We became friends. Once every month I'd visit his
group, the Afro-Americans. In addition to its Prime Minister, the group had other elected leaders, such as the Minister of Education, Minister of Recording, Minister of Justice. I was the Minister of External Affairs. Guests would
drive there with me to contribute their time or influence:
black beauty queens, bankers, financiers, professional
men and women, civil rights workers, teachers, friends.
The inmates they met made a deep impression on the
visitors, and sometimes lasting friendships were formed. I
recall one conversation I had with Dennis Richbow, an
inmate from Detroit who did time in Sandstone and was
later released in Minneapolis, where he earned a new
reputation for perseverance and honesty. It was several
years later, and he was reminiscing with me about the
friends I'd introduced him to since those days in
Sandstone:

"If you want, I'll tell ya. Right? Them folk you been runnin' by me — ya know — they all come at me, one, two, three, at a clip. Gray cats. Brothers. Sisters. They pretty good folk, you know. I mean they serious. Put 'em in your hat and you ain't gonna get rained on. I mean . . . put 'em in a bag, brother, and you gota sack full of sun."

Sandstone is called minimum security. It sprawls across Minnesota's rolling north country, attractive to herds of deer that often graze within a hundred yards of the winding road that approaches the institution. Unlike Stillwater State Prison, whose industrial look and massive stoneworks project permanent hell and damnation, Sandstone reminds me of a military hospital in, say, San Antonio or Anchorage. The low-slung, white, exposed buildings give it a less threatening character than one is conditioned to expect. Tall pines and cottages surrounded by raging flowers offset a tower where a guard greets arriving guests. The tower guard could well have been a forest ranger addressing you over a microphone, but rather than asking if you had polluting tin cans or cigarettes, it was "weapons or narcotics."

Within this "National Preserve" Joe Archie lived and held court. The objective of the Afro-American group was survival. Their curriculum — politics, mathematics, Swahili, history — were subjects whose content was a distant second to the merits of escaping the death sentence of humdrum and boredom. They never minded what they learned as long as there was something to learn, for in the learning they survived.

The prison authorities allowed the Afro-Americans to congregate in an educational setting, but they did not approve because they do not approve survival. Inmates learned how far to push the establishment. Then the establishment became sensitive to how far it could push blacks, and at the end of a day, as in Dow Jones averages, everyone tallied losses and gains. Every day the signals changed, the rules came in on themselves, the games went on, and the way to be smart was to be dumb. As an outsider, I could never recognize Sandstone's posture from one visit to the next.

Joe Archie knew the games as well as any. As a result of his fine handling of the players, he was elected Prime Minister — by a group of blacks who felt that to beat majors and colonels you create a general. He was more than title, however. He was a spirit who moved men to hope and courage. Joe and the Afro-Americans fanned flames in prisons across the land. When Sandstone transferred Joe's ministers from Minnesota to Kansas or Ohio or Pennsylvania, it was like letting rabbits loose in Australia. These prisons soon emulated Sandstone's revolution and renaissance, as black groups became self-help forces.

Joe was not a grandiloquent rhetorician, with much mouth and minimal mind. Joe had simplicity. I did not doubt that he was aware of his skills and received compensation for them when he took his place in the spotlight. He warmed to the secure rays of the sun like any man, and chilled to the shadows. But the simplicity was there long before he came to recognize its impact. He then extended it to a mode of life that influenced as well as inspired others, as Kreisler extended his lyrical violin from satisfaction of self to dramatic hypnosis of audiences. There was depth to him. The pain was in you because you felt Joe Archie was rewarding your life with insight to important lessons. He never solicited your pity. He judged you by what you gave yourself — not by what you could give him. He glued his ideas together with a philosophy of love that transcended color in a prison jungle.

They came from banks and agencies and corporate offices to share in the Sandstone story. They drove the long miles starting at shank of day on traffic-choked highways, and sat for three hours in the Prime Minister's domain. They would be treated to an original play or some swing music, or perhaps to a lesson in Swahili or in African history. And then the speeches. Jimmy Baroka Moyo Scott on Africanism, Kenneth Mwlauma Moses on freedom, Mausa Hall on anger. Then the guests, if they would, spoke. It was usually thanks and gratitude for the inspiring evening. And last, Baridi Mojo Archie. The room . . . forty people . . . would stand in respect as he was announced and went forward. And Joe spoke, quietly. Afterwards, in late darkness, the guests drove south to the Cities in a two-hour religious silence, with the Afro-American program ringing in their consciences and Joe Archie tolling the bell.

It was inevitable, over a period of time, that the visitors would want to do what they could for Joe Archie. Joe was finally released. His parole officer, counselor, and friends persuaded him to stay in Minnesota rather than return home to Illinois. For a few months he lived with my family before finding an apartment nearby. Friends found him a job and a car. He was accepted into the University of Minnesota. He married a local woman who as a result was ostracized by her family. Then he took a better job with an agency called Operation De Novo. His role was counseling first-time offenders who were diverted from lockup after agreeing to enter the agency's program. Director William Henschel claimed that Joe was an excellent employee.

Over this period Joe and I became much closer. We led

our own lives, traveled our own directions, and asked no questions of each other outside the range of comfort and prudence. This gave Joe the freedom of knowing he was not beholden to me as he was to a parole officer. Within our style of relating, we were aware and sensitive to each other's moods and feelings.

It was a delightful summer afternoon in the City of Lakes. Joe and I were sitting on a bench near one of the city's jewels, Lake of the Isles. We watched a child playing nearby and shared a box of Junior Mints, sucking the juices formed by the chocolate drops.

"Never been to college. Hard to believe, Connie . . . hard. Walkin' that campus is no way like Chi. On the South Side I'd be struttin' and hustlin'. Almost half of my life, four-teen years, has been in the joint. This be the longest be-tween busts. No one of them ducks in Chi could see me pullin' parole on a campus."

"How d'ya like it, Joe?"

"Like it? Man I'm ready for likin' anything. Don' know how long I can survive it, but I'm sure likin' it. Hey. I'm like you. Lotsa ways I'm like you. You do all that dreamin' . . . I've watched you. That faraway look in your face, thinkin' of savin' the world, thinkin' of savin' our people, then you get sad, and you don't think you're big enough anymore, and then you move away from it a little. I'm even dreamin'. I wanta save me and make a contribution . . . then I get sad and think it's crazy. I doubt. I move away. Just like you. I know better than anyone . . . a lifetime of experiences . . . better than anyone . . . how to rip off the suckers. I'm an expert on shit and dope. I can make hundreds of green in a night. Right? It's all I know. All I've learned. I get out here and work . . . I'm thankful ya hear . . . but I can make more green in a week than at my job over two birthdays. So I dream that I'll get it together. I'll get it together. But even you give up . . . and you're the main man."

The child was at the lake's edge now. A fish burst up out of the water and plopped down into it again. The child laughed. Then he walked a few feet and the fish, as if knowing which way the child moved, sprung out again. Then again. It was an unreal scene, made for Disney, but happening here before our eyes, a rare experience for us to share.

I broke the spell: "Sandstone has changed my life. It's made me less reckless. I'd be afraid to spend a day in prison. I feel saddened . . . we're in two separate worlds. We're here now, together . . . but God it's brief. You may go back. If you do I could never feel good about visiting you again. And that's so small compared to what it'd be like for you livin' there."

Joe started to interrupt but I went on.

"Shit! Your mother and sister. I made a mistake. I saw them, in Chicago, and they were pleased to see me. But if you had walked into the house they would have been ashamed. I made a mistake. I saw them and found that I was closer to you than they were. Christ, I hated that. I hated getting that reception, as if they were proud of me, as if they could have showed me off. That house. I don't know what I expected, but that house. The furniture was new and expensive and covered with plastic like at my grandmother's. And your sister had beautiful clothes. But the cockroaches, they were all over. I tried to brush one off my neck without embarrassing them. It was that way when I was a kid. I never wanted anyone to see my house. If we ever got rid of those goddamn bugs it would have killed off all the family, too. That filthy city traps your family, Joe. No matter how ashamed of you they are, the city sticks

niggers and cockroaches together. I mean, they're
ashamed of *you*. You . . . when it should be shame for that
city and its mayor and its government."

I sat silent, hunched down against the bench like a
curved twig. Joe looked out over the lake, his legs
stretched a foot beyond mine. The child was leaving, trail-
ing his mother in dogged steps, homeward bound. We sat
in silence a little longer, then we left too.

Joe did well in school and work. There were parties to
attend, and baseball, and meetings with influential citizens. He danced and ice-skated and cross-country skied.
Occasionally we'd speak in tandem at a high school. Joe's
quiet demeanor and powerful presence hypnotized students. He had a way of convincing them that involvement
with narcotics was foolish and unthinkable. A year passed
and all of us talked proud of Joe Archie.

Then cracks in the ice appeared. There were rumors:
"Joe is in trouble." "Joe is into stuff." "Joe is in with the
wrong crowd." "He doesn't want you to know." The pressure was building in him. Every so often I'd see him. His
face was drawn and hollow. We'd look at each other and
communicate beyond words:

"How ya doin' Joe?"

"Real good."

That was all. We were brothers, but neither of us talked. I
knew he loved me more than his family. It was natural for
him to feel he was letting me down, although in the past
we had talked about his right to fail. Some friends would
comment, "How can he do this to himself? He's had every
advantage." One friend was angry with me as well as Joe:
"Goddamn it, Connie, you got me into this!"

Of course I was ashamed. Ashamed of the one or two

who were more worried about their own interests than with the deterioration of this warm human being. They weren't concerned that Joe was inevitably headed back to a life in prison; they were concerned that he had failed them. I knew that Joe was tossed between feeling saddened for his new friends and wanting to be angry at their expectations.

One morning Joe was scheduled to appear in court. He wanted me to be there. It was some sort of preliminary hearing and after it was over, I waited outside the courtroom for him to appear. As in most city halls, assorted characters congregated along the walls: hard-faced women with leopard coats, overweight cops, lawyers sporting dandruff on their coats, pencil-mustached pimps, distraught mothers. Joe came out of the courtroom and we greeted warmly. Four young men and a woman also came up to greet him, all loudly talking at once. I knew they were into junk, and I felt as if they were sucking the blood from Joe's lean body. Somehow, despite my relationship with prisoners and street thugs and gang members, this group was an icy world apart from me. I wanted to punch them out, to destroy them. I wanted to blot them from the land they were poisoning.

"Joe. I got a ride. Do ya need it?"

Joe looked at me. His shoulders were more rounded, his hands deeper into his pants, the eyes submissive and lonely.

"No . . . thanks. I guess I got a ride over here."

"Catch ya next time."

I walked away. My ears heard the loud voices and the street talk, but my back never felt Joe's eyes following me away.

Four treasury men arrested him with stolen checks and

money. He needed to support his habit, so he robbed mailboxes and cashed the contents. They gave him five years at Sandstone Federal Correctional Institution. Judge Larson sentenced him, then chastised Joe like a penitent parochial schoolchild before a prefect of discipline.

"I've received many letters from people who care for you and your welfare. They all speak highly of your skills at your job and with schoolchildren. I think you have let them down. I think that you have used them."

The visiting room at the city jail has a table, two chairs, and an ashtray. We sat across from each other. The marshals hadn't yet picked him up to transfer him north. He was more sure of himself now and his jaw was firm. He wanted me to keep him posted on some personal matters. We talked about our children, about his mother. It was time for me to leave. We hugged, his tall frame strong and dark. My nose was burning and sniffling.

"I love ya, man," he said.

"Right."

One afternoon I met an ex-inmate downtown. We stood and visited awhile, and eventually he asked about Joe. I told him.

"Joe? In the joint? Oh no! What's *wrong* with that man? He had it *all!* He s'pose to *make* it! *Gawwwwwdamn* sonabitch . . . piss me *off*, man!"

I swirled up all the saliva in my mouth and rolled it around, then spit it at his shoes. I took a couple of steps backward looking down at the wet sidewalk, turned about, and jaywalked through a red light.

They got Yard Blacks

and they is bad.

They got Snitch Coons

and they is badder

But House Niggers?

Let me tell ya now –

they is the baddest!

I was asked to appear before a house subcommittee on appropriations. After my talk, one of the committee members, Gary Flakne, took issue with my "indiscriminate" use of the term "house nigger."

A few days later, the Human Rights Department sponsored a very successful legislators' day. Women's groups from around the state put together a program that motivated visitors to jam-pack day and night sessions. That evening, about sixty senators appeared for a cocktail party and dinner. At the dinner, Betty Howard, head of the Women's Division for our department, was sitting with a legislator from western Minnesota. To her, he expressed a certain dislike for me and said he believed he spoke for many others. He also happened to be a member of the appropriations committee and had witnessed the uncomfortable exchange of words between Mr. Flakne and myself.

"May I ask you a question, Mrs. Howard?"

Betty allowed that he might and leaned her head forward to exclude other table guests from the private communication.

"When Commissioner Balfour talks about being a 'house nigger,' does that mean a nigger in the House of Representatives?"

They didn't much like her in the clerical pool

Her glasses were rimmed and she was much too cool

They liked them to "sir" and use protocol

To not say "fuck" or "I like to ball"

But she fooled them all

She said "fuck you sir"

. . . she fooled them all

APRIL

We started to call them Hooverisms. The kind of anecdote or event that swirled around Becky Hoover was sure to cause someone on the staff to repeat it over and over. When she first joined the clerical pool, I think the staff looked down on her. Becky was poor and outspoken and a member of a feminist group and possibly anti-male and anti-world. She was assigned as my appointment secretary, which allowed me the privilege of telling her what I expected of her. It also gave her access to my office, which at times caused minor dissension amongst those who did not have this "privilege." Becky liked me. When my name came up in a women's group meeting, she would bridle if not outright defend me. At times she would enter my office and suggest that I take a course in male chauvinism. Other times she would say, "Ya know, commissioner, you're a lousy administrator, but I love you."

She was the youngest member of the clerical pool, and it drove her crazy. She was constantly in a battle with herself not to tell someone off in that group. Sometimes she did. Then she'd be called on the carpet by the division head, who did a marvelous job of letting Becky's impetuosity run so far before pulling her in.

But she was beautiful. Becky never allowed people to be dishonest with themselves or with her. She saw through the fear and hypocrisy and called them out, one by one by one. If I made a bad decision, Becky would inform me that I blew it. She was usually right, too. Outsiders would recognize her efficiency. At many of my rap sessions with the public, someone would comment about "that Becky in your office."

"Bob Crew is here to see you."
"Thanks, Becky. Send him in."
Bob entered my office and sat before my desk.
"The governor has asked me to tell you that he won't be reappointing you as commissioner. You can have all the time you need to find a new position."
"Thank you, Bob. No surprise."

There were two farewell parties for me. The first was given by a community group. Becky was trying to decide whether or not to go. As she left my office one evening, she tossed off, "Who wants to go to a party for you anyway! Think I'll go home and read a book written by some woman."

The other event was a farewell dinner given by the office staff. She wouldn't go. Her comment was that some of the staff were insincere about how they felt about me and she couldn't stomach sitting with them while they went through the hypocrisy of caring. After the dinner, I went back to the office and found on my desk a gift from Becky — a Turkish opium pipe. The note with it said:

> CB,
> "All good things must end someday,
> autumn leaves must fall,
> but don't you know
> that it hurts me so
> to say good-bye to you."
> –A Summer Song
> Becky

She came in to say good night.

"Thank you. Thank you. Thank you."

"Shut up," she said. "Will you shut up?" Then she cried. And she walked out to her bus and her third-floor apartment and its wall with the love posters and peace signs.

How many fingers have I got up?

One, two, three, or none?

I will not guess for twice I've lost.

You lose again cuz I've got 'em crossed.

You lose three times cuz I've got 'em crossed.

P R O C L A M A T I O N

WHEREAS: the general assembly of the United Nations has adopted a resolution on December 11, 1969 designating 1971 as a special year to focus attention on the problems of racial discrimination throughout the world and called upon human rights leaders in every nation to cooperate in this observance, and

WHEREAS: people in all walks of life had pledged their efforts to work in the elimination of racism and racial discrimination from our national life, and

WHEREAS: nationally recognized groups all over the United States are working to eradicate the fear and hatred that divide America

NOW, THEREFORE, I, Wendell Anderson, Governor of the State of Minnesota, do hereby proclaim the first of April, 1971 as a start of a

YEAR FOR ACTION

to combat racism and racial discrimination and do further call for

A COMMITTMENT FOR BROTHERHOOD

Herein, I urge all agencies of the State of Minnesota and local governments of Minnesota to join in this effort and do further urge the citizens of Minnesota to support those organizations which work for rapid and peaceful social change and bring about brotherhood and the eradication of racism and powerization.

IN WITNESS WHEREOF, I have hereunto set my hand and caused the Great Seal of the State of Minnesota to be affixed at the State Capitol this nineteenth day of March in the year of our Lord one thousand nine hundred and seventy-one and of the State, the one hundred thirteenth.

Wendell R. Anderson
GOVERNOR

●

And that is why minorities never need to read the comic section.

when you see that road

smellin' sweet with tar

sloped graveled sidings

spittin' at your car –

listen to it singin'

ALABAMA, ALABAMA, ALABAMA ROAD

WISHIN' I COULD CARRY FRED AND WILLIE'S LOAD

singin'

WISHIN' I COULD CARRY FRED AND WILLIE'S LOAD

The car seemed to crawl ahead. It was forty miles to Panama City. The night, warm and moonless and aromatic, was a transparent curtain for my fears. Dave Helman was relaxed as he drove, holding to the Florida speed limit, a counterbalance to me, his passenger. His voice came easy and strong: "It's okay. When something's gonna screw up I can feel it in the back of my neck. It's fine. No danger. Not tonight."

We were fleeing (I exaggerate — Dave would call it "departing") Port St. Joe, a town of five thousand on the Gulf of Mexico, to our Holiday Inn in Panama City. We had just gathered forty signatures from black residents declaring that Port St. Joe was too discriminatory for blacks to receive a fair trial there. Two blacks, Wilbert Lee and Freddie Pitts, were on death row for a double murder they did not commit, and their case was up for retrial in Port St. Joe. But their lawyers felt they would never get a fair trial there. They were trying to get a change of venue, and for that, the signatures we carried would help. This was 1971, but for Pitts and Lee it had been a long struggle, starting eight years before.

On a hot night in 1963, a group of blacks drove to the Mo-Jo gas station to place a phone call. They returned to Port St. Joe and socialized well into the morning. At dawn the sheriff was alerted that the two gas station attendants were missing. He picked up the visitors of the night before and interrogated them. Two days later the attendants were found dead, bullets in their heads. One of the black women in the group, Willie Mae Lee, following extensive questioning, accused two of her companions of the crime. As a result, Pitts and Lee were jailed and eventually sentenced to death by the electric chair.

Sixteen days after the Mo-Jo incident, Curtis Adams, Jr., a white man, robbed and murdered a gas station attendant near Ft. Lauderdale. A few months passed before Adams was arrested, but for another crime — robbing a finance company — and sentenced to prison. Two years later, Adams confessed to the Ft. Lauderdale murder as well as the Mo-Jo gas station slayings. Eight years following the crime, the Florida Supreme Court granted a new trial to Pitts and Lee.

The Pitts-Lee case was brought to national attention when Gene Miller, Pulitzer Prize winning journalist from the Miami *Herald*, became interested in it and gave it

138

much publicity in his paper. He is also writing a book on the case, which is full of strange coincidences and bizarre highlights:

1. Pitts and Lee confessed to the double murder, then retracted the confession, claiming threats and intimidations.

2. When Pitts and Lee retracted their confessions, a police official ran out into the street shouting, "I'll get the confession! I know how to handle niggers!"

3. Two army investigators (Pitts was a private in the U.S. Army) were delayed from seeing Pitts for eight days. They were sent to another county and another jail on a wild-goose chase. When they finally tracked him down, they found him with a bruised head and swollen jaw. Both investigators feared for their own safety as well.

4. Pitts wrote to Jack Winick, a lieutenant in the army stationed at New Orleans, for legal counsel. Winick was soon taken off the case by military authorities, who stated, "You'll antagonize the whites in the area."

5. Miami attorneys for Pitts and Lee found spikes under the tires of their car and needed police protection whenever they visited their clients in Port St. Joe.

6. Willie Mae Lee's testimony changed in content three times. She claimed that the suspects beat the victims with a tire iron, but an autopsy showed nothing.

7. There was no physical evidence linked to the suspects such as a gun or fingerprints. The state contended that they had plaster casts of their footprints, but when confronted to produce them, never did.

8. Reporter Gene Miller was beaten up on the courthouse steps in Port St. Joe. No action was taken by local authorities.

9. W. Fred Turner, the court-appointed attorney, en-

couraged Pitts and Lee to throw themselves at the mercy of the jury. They did and were sentenced to the electric chair — on the same day that Martin Luther King was addressing thousands in Washington, D.C., about his dream of "freedom at last."

10. The jury was all white.

Jack Winick, the army lieutenant contacted by Pitts and now an attorney in Minneapolis, called to acquaint me with the Pitts-Lee case. He explained that the case was up for retrial, and that in order for the accused to get a change of venue, local blacks must sign a petition indicating that need. So far, locals were justifiably frightened of southern retaliation and would not cooperate. He suggested that a national figure might be successful in motivating people to sign, and asked if I would be willing to call some black leaders and enlist their aid. Jack had been in constant touch with Freddie Pitts, and the two of them had great respect for each other. He as well as others who touched this tragedy did all they could to contribute to Pitts's and Lee's freedom.

I soon became a party to Jack's frustration. My calls to established black leaders were unfulfilling. Jesse Jackson of Operation Breadbasket was impossible to reach. Roy Wilkins of the NAACP never returned my numerous calls. Rev. Ralph Abernathy was out of town, and Julian Bond's secretary in Atlanta informed me that Mr. Bond was tied up for two years. It was obvious that I was inadequate and without proper influence for this assignment. I called Jack Winick and told him the disheartening news.

"Why don't you go down?"

"Me?" I was incredulous. "I'm no national figure. What can I do?"

"Go." Jack wasted no breath. "I'll call Ted Bowers and Irwin Block."

Irwin Block was a Miami attorney who dedicated his services to freeing Pitts and Lee at no charge. Ted Bowers was a black lawyer in Panama City who acted as a spokesman for the blacks in Port St. Joe. A few days later I had a roundtrip ticket to Panama City.

The Holiday Inn rested easily on a warm Gulf where waters bathed the piles and sea walls with patient caresses. The white sands and terns eased away the northern tensions that damp winds and cold temperatures tend to lodge in one's back muscles. But before I had a chance to stroll the coastline, a knock on my door announced the entrance of Dave Helman, a detective who had been assigned to go with me to Port St. Joe. We set out to find Ted Bowers.

Bowers was a pleasant, young, constantly smiling black who greeted us warmly and seemed genuinely grateful that we were there. He said he was setting up a meeting for us in Port St. Joe the next day, where hopefully we could collect the proper number of signatures.

The following morning Dave and I set out for Port St. Joe, forty miles east along the coastline. Dave briefed me on procedures: "I'm a notary public. We'll go to D Street and ask for Bowers's contact. You explain to him what we want. I have newspaper clippings of the Pitts-Lee trial. Ask people to read them so that they can be fully aware of the facts. Then they sign the petition, right? I'll stamp them to make them official. We need as many as possible."

He cleared his throat. "Now I've got two missions. One is to interview local whites in this county. Find out what they think of the trial. Most feel they are guilty, I know that. I'll try to get them to sign a statement to that effect. It can show a prejudiced community. A jury from here would hurt. Irwin Block can use prejudiced statements like that for a change of venue as well as the ones you're trying for. The second reason for me to be here is to protect you. Look."

He pulled a gun from beneath the dashboard, brandished it, then replaced it. "There's another one in the crease of the seat. Have to fold it back to get at it."

He pointed to a toggle switch below the dash. "When I hit that, it sets off a tape recorder in the trunk. If anyone stops me I can tape him."

D Street was submerged in squinting sunlight. Dave's dusty car glided to a stop before a rustic grocery store. The lady there said we could find our contact, Sam Stallworth, at the next corner. We walked over to a pool hall where Sam greeted us cordially before escorting us to a back room. Five young men were waiting there. They knew the murder story well and never hesitated as they signed our affidavits. I was surprised at the absence of reserve. Dave's face gave no indication of his emotions. He patted each sheet with a notary stamp and we were done.

"Are there any others who can sign?" I asked.

Sam smiled and answered, "C'mon. We'll go next door."

We followed him silently into the street, the sun blinding in contrast to the cool indoors of the wooden buildings. In a bar up the street we took our places at a table and were offered cool glasses of 7-Up.

"Got maybe three more here," Sam said. "Jake. You wanna get on this? It's for Pitts and Lee. Bowers says it's okay."

While Dave tapped the three new sheets of paper with the metal stamp, I asked the small group how we could get the town involved. "Appreciate what you're doing, but to do us any real good we need at least twenty to thirty more. Can we come back, have a meeting, somethin' like that? Maybe spread the word?"

One of the men looked at the others. The faces showed agreement. It was okay. We decided to return the next evening. I felt puffed with elation — it seemed so easy — when one of the men put a hand on my shoulder.

"You can't leave yet, Mr. Balfour. There a police officer out there. Look like he visiting some of the folk. He a colored man, but not one to trust. Wouldn't do for you to go out there just yet."

"Damn!" cursed Dave. "My car! The plate shows it's from Dade County!"

"Well, you just hold calm now. We'll just see what do happen." The man was round-faced and large in the shoulders. He walked around the counter and began to wipe a drinking glass with a yellow cloth, looked at it with the eye of a diamond dealer, put it down softly and selected another, peered at it, and silently started polishing the clear tumbler. No sound registered in the shadows of the bar. A juke box crouched at rest . . . an electric clock ran silent above the bar . . . no chair creaked. The man at the wooden bar set more glasses, top down, upon a folded towel. He finally wiped his fingers and looked up, his eyes making a careful study of the street beyond. I followed his direction and saw dust settling across the street and to the corner. The officer had driven away. In a few moments we did the same.

I had nothing to do the next day. It would be evening before I'd call Port St. Joe for information on our next meeting place and time. Dave watched me wade in the retreating tide, the salt water plopping around my ankles as I kicked at phantom sea dragons. My guardian reclined in a peppermint beach chair, his eyes sleepily following my childish play. I ran across the beach, twenty short yards to a retaining sea wall, and back. Kicking sand up my calves and shins, I pounced into more inches of ocean, deep-knee-bended to my toes, and stroked the sand down. Then I goose-stepped to the wall again, back and forth, the sand thumping below the smack of each heel. Dave never moved except for a smile around his lips. His chin down on his chest folded in plateaus and his dark skin broke no perspiration.

A dark, delicate bird — maybe a tern — stood motionless on the wooden sea wall.

"Watch me, Davey! I'm gonna walk up real close to 'er!"

I took a step. Slow. Another. Another. It looked straight ahead, out to sea, no feather moving in the Florida breeze, no eyelid descending across the cold cornea. My steps were silent, the sand breaking gently quiet beneath my almost flat arches. The tern seemed to grow larger. It should have flown off. Now. It should be on its way. But the creature stayed. I watched it more intently now, my body frozen like a photograph of a walking figure. We were mere feet apart from the beat of each other's heart . . . the two of us, both from the same world, both needing the mystery of the sea and the warmth of the sand. And then it moved. A spidery leg . . . just barely moved. The play of living cells moved up and into a base of charcoal feathers and, like a miniature awning, the wings opened and reached for sky and height as all of the tern lifted off from its prints in the sand. I watched its flight along the length of beach and then felt the strain of weary muscles ease as I relaxed. I turned, and Dave was reclining as before, his chin on his chest, his smile now gone, his eyes on my face like an old child.

That evening I called Port St. Joe. A minister's son who was to meet with us was out of town. His father wouldn't come to the phone. A gas station attendant who was in the group could not be reached. Another contact was visiting a relative up in Georgia. One by one, the young men we had met the day before turned up missing. Even Ted Bowers, who was planning to drive over to Port St. Joe with us, had not yet returned from a meeting in a nearby town. We didn't know what to do, where to go for advice. Finally I called Ted's secretary at home and implored her to suggest someone who would cooperate with us.

"Call Adele Jackson. She's a grandmother and not afraid of anybody."

Adele was just that. On the phone she expressed concern and apologized for my trouble.

"Can you be at the Reverend Stallworth's Baptist Church? I'll have God-lovin' folk there."

The Baptist Church looked over a dusty road crowded with old cars and pickup trucks. Dave commented, "Looks like real people are here."

We walked through an open door into the odor of dry wood and a setting of simplicity. Standard pews with short backs and tucked-in hymnals were supporting about sixty elderly men and women. An attractive lady smilingly moved toward us.

"I'm Mrs. Jackson. Welcome."

She led us to the altar steps where Dave deposited his briefcase containing newspapers, stamp and pad, pens, and petition sheets. The townspeople sat quietly, watching Dave sort his articles on the top step. I tried to find young people in the group, but there were none. I wondered if they'd really sign the petitions. I wondered if I would, if I lived in this Gulf town.

"Thank you for coming. My name is Conrad Balfour. This is my friend Dave Helman. I come from Minnesota. It will be worth my trip if we can get together and help two men who need all of us more than ever. You've lived with this story for eight years now, and I can imagine how it's festering inside you. You've never had a role to play before, but tonight, there is something you can do. You and I have a chance, a small chance maybe, to assist in freeing Freddie Pitts and Wilbert Lee. White people think they are guilty, although there are some who know they are innocent. The real killer knows they are innocent. The law knows they are innocent. And you know they are innocent. If enough of you say that a black man cannot get a fair trial in this community, the lawyers have a good chance of convincing a court to transfer the trial to a new location. It's that simple. Your signatures. Tonight. And maybe Pitts and Lee can go free. But not only Pitts and Lee. I think that you must sign for yourselves. I think that you must declare to each other that no innocent brother of yours will ever again walk alone. It won't stop job dismissals. It might not stop intimidation, and it might even provoke physical hurt. Maybe. But slavery will come to a halt here in Port St. Joe, and all of you will be able to scribble in your Bibles your own emancipation . . . dated, 1971."

No one stirred. Perspiration broke out on some brows, but no paper fans showed. The contrast in color jarred my eyes . . . earthy black faces next to gray and white hair. They were beautiful to me. They would sign. I knew they would sign.

The newspaper clippings were distributed, and they read them, every word of them, as if they were seeing them for the first time, as if they were matching the print with the indelible traces in their memories. Then they began to sign. One sheet . . . one signature. Dave moved about the pews rapping each petition with his notary public stamp.

It was time to leave and silently I embraced some of the members. Mrs. Jackson urged us to hurry. "You must leave. It's dark, and you must not be here after dark." I thanked and hugged her, and left Port St. Joe forever.

The lawyers for Pitts and Lee won their plea for a change of venue, but they lost any hope for a fair trial. The judge designated the town of Marianna, Florida, as the new location. Marianna is about one hundred miles north of St. Joe, part of the Florida panhandle, and as volatile as its sister city. A trial in Marianna was likely to be a repeat performance of the one that was held in Port St. Joe eight long years ago. Irwin Block's law firm wanted another change of venue. They needed five hundred signatures this time. If they could try this case outside the Florida panhandle — Miami or even Talahassee — Pitts and Lee would go free. No court would be so blind to the strong evidence showing the innocence of these two men. No court except those in Gulf and Jackson counties.

Once again I was asked to help obtain the needed signatures. Soon I was on my way to Marianna, with a quick stopover in Miami to confer with Gene Miller and Irwin Block.

The blacks in Marianna were eager. They felt that for the first time their community was standing up to the establishment. It took little labor on my part to get the job accomplished — the signatures came easy.

The highlight for me was when I finally met Freddie and

Wilbert. They were in the Marianna jailhouse awaiting the new trial, and I was allowed to visit with them briefly. Freddie held my hand a moment and expressed his thanks.

"Everything is going okay. We're doin' fine. Heard you were around. Just be cool. How's Winick? Tell him I was asking. And tell him to write. He owes me."

Wilbert was interested in Minneapolis. He had hopes of living there when released. "Must be a fine town." A few minutes more and it was time to separate. I felt their anguish and their brave attempt to present a bold front.

Five hundred signatures were delivered to Irwin Block. Gene Miller wrote to me in Minneapolis and said that white citizens of Marianna had marched through town protesting the efforts to free Freddie and Wilbert. A cloth dummy had been hanged in effigy, crumpled and lifeless, with a breast sign showing the words "fucking nigger."

The court denied a change of venue. The judge informed the defense that Marianna knew little of the crime. In the winter of 1972, Freddie Pitts and Wilbert Lee were tried and found guilty of a double murder, and for the second time in their lives were sentenced to death by the electric chair.

Freddie writes now. He writes of watered-down milk and cereal and hard, stale bread. Of an exercise yard no larger than a child's sandbox. He writes of having to strip naked following each visit from his attorney or after each return from the yard . . . the wing officer looking in each man's mouth, under each man's raised arms, and then, as the prisoners turn away from the officer and bend over from the waist, opening their butts with cold fingers. Two. Three. Four times a day. Every day. Every week. Every day of every week. Freddie says, "It's cleaner between my black butts than in the halls of justice."

Little bird white

you died last night

and heaven awaits you today.

Thank you sweet Lord

but don't bare your sword

if I fly a different way.

CHRISTIE

W hat could you say? "Go home and get changed into something normal"? Or, "Are you for real?" She was a sight. Purple net stockings. Kelly green blouse. Long blond hair matching yellow ballet slippers. The colors fought and scrambled at each other. After all, she *was* nineteen — the age was late for missing obvious dress techniques. Every day she'd wander into the office . . . a myriad, wanting in taste, short on wardrobe. Every day after she arrived I'd realize that the air was fresher. After she darted into my corner of the building, I was happier and more relaxed and much more alive.

Her name was Christie. And her clothes didn't matter. Not to me, not to the director, Stan King, not to anyone on the staff of the Twin Cities Opportunities Industrialization Center. We loved her and protected her. At least we tried. Her mother still lived, but Christie bummed around from one friend's living room to another's porch. Her father was dead. She hated him. Real hate. He had used chains on her skin and she could never forget the beatings. Somehow, through all that, her physical beauty was never marred. The hair was brilliant gold rushing well below pretty shoulders. Her face was flowers. And it was flawless . . . new-fallen snow untouched by scar or weather, unravaged by pock or liquid-filled pimple. The eyes were blue and rarely warm. Her walk was tomboy.

Christie always needed a stake for a meal. She never begged. You knew. Christie was going to be hungry in an hour because you would be hungry in an hour, and someone would see that grub money was available. Our self-help program helped train and place many beautiful people, but she was special. No one bothered to analyze why. Maybe it was the way she haunted us with her childlike beauty. She looked years younger than her age. You wanted to take her home and tuck her in with a doll. Whatever it was, it worked like magic. It worked in spite of ceaseless chattering and incandescent fashions. Christie was charismatic; Christie was beautiful. For the rest of my life I would remember her and the profound impact she made on me.

We got to know each other better. I discovered that Christie was brutally honest and candid. It was a quality that allowed little room for hypocrisy and double-talk in her presence. When I slipped into insincerities, she would halt me with a glacial stare or a four-letter obscenity.

From time to time, Christie would stay at my home; this was one way she could escape pressure from her world. It's possible that she was one of the world's leading narcissists. She could spend a day preening before her mirror, jutting a perfect jaw obliquely from left to right until the indigo eyes strained to bend their vision around the gentle curves of her face. That face. So beautiful. She didn't believe that, though. Her faith was in her makeup. Eyebrows and cheeks would receive painstaking care and attention from fingers trained in hundreds of hours of applying modern camouflage. She needed this finger and eye action — even the pure narcissist can grow drowsy from mirror reflections that give back no physical contact. "Do I look okay to you?" It was a plea, really. As she inquired, the eyes were constantly inspecting for interruptions on the smoothness of her neck. Then, the decision made, she would quickly grasp a brush and begin to stroke her hair. I was never allowed to aid in this ritual. "You might damage some endings." I was satisfied to watch, for it was a joy to see the hair come alive under the twist of hand and wrist. The room would transform to the sounds of her brushing as it played out rhapsodies and lullabies. Her neck and back would sway to the rhythm of her humming golden hair. It lulled me as it did her. When the final stroke of the plastic wand departed from the silken strands, she would rest her back to the chair and smile at me.

"How are you? Are you eating well? Let me fix some scrambled eggs."

This was patience's reward.

Christie dropped out of our lives often. Six months might pass and not a word. I'd worry and hope she was safe. When I gave up seeing her again she'd call. Her eyes were weak and she rarely read newspapers, but someone would mention that my name was printed somewhere, and "how was I?" Usually she was with a new girlfriend or an old girlfriend. We'd meet at one of her hangouts and she'd show me off to all her drinking companions. Her pride in knowing me was genuine. Still, I was always uncomfortable and eventually she would rescue me with a firm exit and a talkative ride by the lakes. A few days would go by and Christie would fall from sight for another terribly long period of time.

It was one of those days when she had no wish to "go on." There was nothing I could say to pull her out of the blues. That evening I was to give a talk to some students at St. Olaf College; they had requested that I speak on homosexuality.

"Why don't you come along, Chris?"

She sparked. "That would be great! Are you sure I won't be in the way?"

"Of course not. Have you ever spoken to a group before? Maybe you could speak on the same program."

"What would I say? Jesus Christ!"

"I don't know. Tell them how it feels to be you. Why not? If it's an uptight audience we should swap roles. God! That's not bad!"

She listened suspiciously as I continued. "I'll say that I'm bisexual. You can be straight. It should be simple to sell. Right? We'll give them a chance to touch us. Some will be repulsed by me."

"I don't want people to touch *me!*" She said it painfully.

"You can pull it off. They'll love touching you. You're apple-cheeked and the girl next door."

"Yah. They'll *love* touching me. It's *me* who's uptight, stupe!"

"Try, Christie. Will you? There are people out there who will never understand you. Who knows. This might pull 'em around."

Although the idea was threatening to her, she agreed to do it. The role-swapping wasn't necessary after all — the group was young and hip and aware. Christie had felt threatened, not because people might get into her head, but because they just might embrace her skin-to-skin. She had difficulty even when I hugged her. My arms would circle her waist and she'd tense. Rarely would she respond with her arms anywhere but at her sides. If I kissed her she'd stiffen her head. Sometimes she'd curse.

"Jesus Christ, Conrad! Jesus Christ Amen!"

A moan would spill out from between her teeth.

"Eeeeeaah! Eeeeeaah!"

Something like an ignition key trying to turn over a cold Minnesota Ford engine. Her cry signaled pain and distaste and frustration. Only when I retreated could she regain her cool composure.

The next time I saw Christie, she took me to a coffee and sandwich place she knew called The Club. A narrow staircase led to its front entrance, where a handsome college type collected a dollar admission. A back room had tables and net candles with a corner juke. The center section was kitchen and counter space to pick up orders. The front room was a duplicate of the back.

We arrived there close to midnight and selected a table up front. There were only a few other customers. Christie was the only woman. Two young men had popped their heads in once or twice and nodded in detached recognition. At 12:30 they came in again and made their way to the jukebox. The money deposited, they both froze into dancing positions awaiting the first note of their selection . . . like milers at the starting line, waiting to perform their melody of motion on signal from the pistoled conductor. Three Dog Night erupted from the neon speaker with "Joy to the World." The youths went into an incredible dance

that hypnotized me for three minutes of jumping sound.
We were sitting directly opposite the music box. The
space for dancing was small, just a few square feet. Intimate. With their backs to the box the couple gyrated and
pranced up to our table. Then in staccato stamp, they
militantly halted forward motion and retreated to the starting point, clicked their heels, and advanced on us again.
Both wore long-sleeved colored shirts puffed at the wrists
and open up the front. Both were devastatingly handsome.
Their rapid movements kept the table candles ghosting
shadows on the low ceiling. The seated onlookers picked
automatically at baskets of chips. I tapped my foot. Christie was excited and held her hands alternately to her
mouth and to her head. The dancers had their arms around
each other. One looked with false nonchalance to the ceiling, his long locks popping up and back like hot pancake
batter. The other watched his feet with intensity. The
music at that time was thrilling millions. Here, tonight, it
belonged only to a couple of youthful dancers. They had
bandited the beat, the words, the melody, and had made
the song their own. Now the music was driving to its
throbbing conclusion. The dancers pirouetted clockwise,
ending in fencing pose. Face to face. Lithe. Steady. Frozen.
We waited. Finally they eased into relaxed smiles and
walked out of the room. I breathed again and reached for
Christie's hand.

By 2 P.M., The Club was heavy with customers. Christie
was table-hopping, weaving her personable thread into a
carpet of togetherness. A Spaniard had joined the group,
and was standing in the room's center telling a short funny
story. Everyone laughed. He would visit a table and talk
loud enough for all to hear. Then he'd go to the next table
and tell more funny stories and the room would rock with

good-natured laughter. Often he'd sit on someone's knee and peck a kiss on his cheek. Christie paid rapt attention and it was clear she was enjoying herself. As the crowd thinned out, the few remaining considered going out to eat at another restaurant. The Spaniard was asked for his opinion. It was obvious that his popularity dictated whether the Embers or the Chestnut Tree would be the place to go for this late night eating excursion.

"Go to the Embers? I went to the Embers once. It screwed up my undying flame for you, m'luv." They all laughed. I couldn't figure the humor. "You laugh at me? I laughed once. It screwed up my tonsils." They broke into torrents this time. "Hey! That's a neat belt you're wearing, Bobby. I wore a neat belt once. It screwed up my love life." Laughter. "I had a love life once. But my wife got into the act. I had a wife once. But he ran away with my attorney. I had an attorney once. But he had a crush on me and my wife got jealous and returned. Really screwed me up that time."

I decided that the uproarious laughter was not a response to any clever humor so much as a recognition of the feeling they had for their popular friend. For the first time now, the Spaniard looked at me and tossed a friendly smile. Then he risked sitting on my lap. I had been the only male exempt from his flirting up to then. He kissed me on the cheek, testing. I reacted neutrally, feeling the pressure of the trial. His brown eyes burned into my soul, and I read every word they were silently shouting:

CONRAD BALFOUR ... CHAMPION OF THE UNDER-DOG. HOW DO YOU FEEL WHEN IT'S FINALLY PUT TO YOU, BABY? WELL, HERE YOU ARE, BIG SHIT, REJECT IT. GO AHEAD. REJECT IT. SHOW US THAT YOU ARE AS FULL OF SHIT AS THE REST OF THOSE PRICKS OUT THERE.

"Do you want to go? The Embers?"

"No, I don't, but thanks." I smiled.

"You're okay," he said. "I know where you're at."

He got up off my knee and walked out, followed by his entourage of laughing admirers.

She wore a light blue robe. After washing and brushing her teeth, she crawled under a too-small blanket and snuggled into the couch.

"You can rest too."

I rested my head on her bare feet and fell asleep.

The next night I rested my head on her belly, my legs dangling over the arm rest. Somehow I slept comfortably.

One night I asked her how she felt about a man sleeping so close to her.

"It's all right, I guess. I dunno. I miss Jackie. I know I bug her. But I do miss her. That's one thing about you. You don't bug me. I tried it once with a guy. He was all over me. UGH! What goddamn hands! I love women. They are one of the few happinesses I have. I love you too, Connie. I know that you understand. When I first met you, Jesus Christ, I thought you'd never shut up! These moments are nice, though. Too bad they'll last for such a little time. I think that's sad. When I'm ready for you to touch me, I'll let you know. I've got signals. If you want to turn me off, Christ, just push me!"

She rambled on. Slow. Eyes closed. Relaxed.

"I love the sweetness of women's thighs. We're more gentle with our touching. A woman has a way that's special, I think. Double it with two of us and the gentleness would comfort a world made of eggshell. The beauty can't be matched. Can you understand? The soft doubles. The breasts double. The buttocks. I'm happy with that. Happy."

She fell asleep.

Each night she wore her pretty robe. Each night she retired in beauty and each morning awakened in it. On this night she asked me if I wanted her to leave off her robe. I nodded. She dropped it on the floor and put herself on the couch. My eyes still see Christie in her nakedness. I can't describe that to you. I don't know how. This lovely woman demonstrated beauty far beyond curve and hollow. Her comfort in disrobing. The trust, the ease, the love. This was the real beauty and the miracle. She held me to her breasts and I wandered slowly into slumber.

The next evening Christie was gone. It was another year before I was to see her again. My mother was staying with me then, living out the last days of her life in our apartment on Lake Calhoun. Christie, I learned, was living with five women in a two-story white cottage in Richfield. They knew nothing about her, they all worked except for Christie, and all attended the same church. Sometimes Christie tagged along for evening services and even seemed to like it.

I picked her up and we drove to my apartment so she could meet my mother. On the way over we got up-to-date on each other's activities.

"I've found God."

"What?"

She squinted at me, not wanting to repeat herself, then looked wistfully away and said, "I've found God."

"Is it your roommates?"

"I guess. They're all so happy and sincere. When I go to their church I feel better than anything. You know what I mean?"

"I notice something different," I said. "I think it's the swearing. And you do look well."

"I'm at peace. For the first time I'm at peace. I clean the house and do some little things and I dunno. They're nice, Connie. Real, real nice."

"Then they don't force church on you?"

"Aw hell! No way! I go because I want to. I've always believed in God anyway. Didn't you know that? He's the only one who can put it together for you. I think of you, Connie. Honest to God. I'd be absolutely complete if you were happy, too."

"Christie, it ain't all that bad."

She looked out again. Lake Harriet was a diamond. My apartment was just a few minutes away with a silent mother to introduce and a refrigerator full of Coke and sherbert.

"Connie. Will you help me?"

It was another plea.

"Yes, of course."

"I'd like to leave this world." The voice was small and thin and distant. "I'd like to meet HIM. I'm so much at peace. So happy. I'm not afraid anymore."

"Christie?" It was said as a question. I waited for rescue. How could I help? What would she ask?

"I don't want to be alone when it happens. Could I be with . . . you? It's terrible. To be alone, I mean. That's all that frightens me. Not to die. I know I wouldn't have a problem. But . . . to be by myself . . . I couldn't. Just couldn't."

"I can't, sweetheart."

Her voice rose. "But whyyyy?"

"I don't know why. It's too sudden. I . . . I can't anyway."

"Fine. Okay. Fine. But why?" she challenged.

I stumbled around, looking for a reason to convince her that I didn't need a reason. She interrupted my thoughts. "I'm not asking as much as you think. I have a right to believe in God. A right to be an atheist. You've said that. I have a right to live. Why not to die? Who has the moral authority to deny me a decision on my own life? If I were a man and in the army I could die in some stinking war! Don't you think that of all the jocks done in over there — that they were killed cuz Uncle Sam sacrificed their lives? He has the right to send boys out to die — young boys, old men. He's making a decision on other people's destinies. I say that I have more right than he or anyone else. A decision on *my* life! Christ, it's MY life! Mine at eighteen! Mine at sixty-two!

"What will they do to me? Inspire me to live with sermons and incense? Put me in a home with straightjackets and serums? Keep me in misery so that I live the rest of my life as a vegetable? C'mon. You're not pulling any trigger or releasing the gas. You've been a part of my life. I'm inviting you to be near me at my happiest moment . . . when I go to meet my God.

"My robe. That will be nice. I need some pills. Please help me. Will you?"

I didn't answer. I thought of the papers and the newsmen asking questions and the hate letters and the phone calls. I thought and thought and I could not answer. The car pulled into the parking lot and we did not talk until I opened the apartment door to greet my mother.

Mom was sitting in a soft chair next to the television. Christie went over to her and talked her into drinking something like Coke or milk. Mom and I kissed, then I sprawled to the floor tired and confused. Half of me was listening to the television and the other to the sounds of

Christie waiting on my mother. She had put a full Coke into Mom's hand and Mom dropped it, spilling it on the carpet. Christie placed another in her hand and again she dropped it. The third time Mom earned a lecture on how to hold a small green Coca Cola bottle; this time there was no incident. I drifted off, forgetting everything, contented in the peace of the apartment.

Soon I became aware of a pressure on my shoulder. It was Christie snuggling into the harbor of my chest and arm. The sound of sobbing joined the low volume of Channel 11. Her tears patted my skin and stayed cool against it. As I looked for the cause of this concern, my eyes traveled to Mom, her quiet form sitting in the chair before me. Her brown eyes were wide and unblinking and full with tears. She was fastened with gaze to Christie. The young woman. Beautiful, healthy, with the opportunity to live — and the choice was eternal rest. The older lady. Beautiful. Unhealthy. The desire to live . . . yet the choice was already taken away. Eternal rest.

They had reached each other. In some mystical way they had communicated. The tears from Mom's eyes slipped down her cheeks, parting the brown skin into sections of wet and dry. Christie pulled herself to a sitting position, her arms embracing her knees. Then they hugged. And we left. Christie and I. We left. Quiet. I forgot about reasons and newspapers and jails and fines and Catholic damnation. She looked my way . . . a half smile.

"Okay?" she asked.

"Yes, Christie," I smiled in response. "It's okay."

Buck. Buck.

How many fingers have I got up?

Buck? Hey . . . Buck . . . . . . ?

GEORGE

Across the river was Harvard University and the Massachusetts Institute of Technology. It was night and we could see other buildings lining the Charles River, none of them identified now. There was a bridge, too, holding the cities together . . . Cambridge, Boston . . . like a surgeon's metal clamp keeping wounded skin tight-pressed for the coming sutures. And there were lights. The cool air floated waves of currents up to the edges of the glow as if to keep its frosty fingers warm. The sky held some day yet. On this night it could not completely shake off twilight from its coat of black.

But there was night enough for the room. The room. High above Back Bay's Jewish delicatessens and yellow taxis and naked Christmas tree. Shadows played in hushed glides across the wall. She could see my face, I knew . . . she could feel me tremble. Those times that pain walked out from within my body she'd ask, and if she tugged with more strength than what I had to resist, she would discover my hiding places. But she'd ask first. It was good, but it would have to get better. On this night I must talk with her *before* the questions formed. I must start to show her that I was willing to share now, that I want to share now. Either way the tears would slip across to her cotton nightgown. Either way I would tense with fear and puzzled despair.

"I want to leave Boston. I want us to fly back. God."

Mary held me tightly now. Her whisper was gentle. "Are you afraid?"

"Yes. Yes. I'm always afraid. Every year I visited this city, before they all had died. Grandmother. Edmund. Ruby. I loved them. I know. But I'm so smothered. Depressed. You know? I'd stay with them for awhile, then go downtown and see a movie — alone. I'd walk the streets . . . the corner where we hung out. No one was ever there. They're all gone." The tears were with us now. "When I was growing I felt trapped in Boston. Never thought I'd get anyplace at all. Then I left and it was okay. Damn. I dunno. Each time I come back here I'm lonely and afraid."

"How about this time?" She was crying gently as she asked.

"I don't want to go through with it. I DON'T WANT TO TALK WITH GEORGE! OH MARY, I DON'T. I DON'T!"

She held my head to her face and chin and neck and shoulder. Our tears joined and mixed and ran in single convolution.

"I love you," she said. "It's good that you show fear. You never show it. Tomorrow will come, but tonight I'm closer to you than ever."

The morning slipped into town cloudy gray. Across the Charles, MIT was stark white against the horizon. It was 1972 and my forty-fourth Thanksgiving, but only the first that the choice was ours — Mary's and mine — to make. I had suggested to her that we call my Uncle George in Boston and spend Thanksgiving with them. George and his wife Lorraine were delighted that we were coming, and we were looking forward to it, too. But when the plane left

Minneapolis, I grew morose and withdrawn. By the time we landed in Boston, I felt ill. Mary immediately sensed it was more than a physical problem.

We slept late on Thanksgiving morning. George would soon be coming for us. George was sixty-seven years old. His body was strong even now, and his face was loaded to the pores with self-discipline and power. Lorraine was sixty-two, but they both looked much younger. In the thirty years I had known Lorraine, she was unswervable — always gentle and delicate and unalterably patient. They lived in Roxbury, a black section of the city that housed poverty programs, urban decay, and crime. It was the same to me now as it was thirty years ago. George would say, "You can't dress up an old lady."

George and Lorraine ran a small tailor shop on Tremont Street. He would leave the house at 5 A.M. to open for business, starting the day pressing and tagging. Lorraine took the bus at 8 A.M. to join him for a day of sewing and mending. Tremont Street was a junkyard — a collection of dusty brick tenements whose storefronts were occasionally tenanted by a barber shop or liquor store. Across from the tailor shop was Slade's, once a delicious fried chicken haven that attracted Boston's posh crowd. Now it was only a crumbling shell of its glorious past.

"I knew that you wanted to talk. Yeeees. I *told* Lorraine, 'Conrad is going to want to talk.' I wondered when, heh, heh. Thought maybe, maybe the last time you came . . . when Ruby was sick. But I'm glad you're askin' now. Uh huh."

We were sitting in their living room. Mary and Lorraine had been in the kitchen earlier, preparing the meal and getting acquainted. Later, Mary told me she had alerted

Lorraine that I would confront George on my past. Lorraine had said, "I don't think George knows any more than Conrad does. That family never asked questions."

"What do you know of my dad, George?"

"I really don't know. I dunno. I dunno. They'd never tell me. You knew — you just knew — that you wasn't s'posed to nose around. Least of all me. I wasn't the favored lamb. That was Ruby, you know. I was working at Sears then. Came home from work one day and here's Ruby in the house with a baby. I asked her who it was, and she says it's just a friend's. I never said anymore. Never asked another question. Of course I suspected, you know. I suspected. And I was dead certain when one day I came in on her and she was breast feedin' you. I didn't ask and she didn't explain. They said your dad was an Englishman. Garth Balfour. But I never saw his picture or a letter or heard a telephone call."

"Yes," I responded. "Ruby said he was from a titled family — a baron. That he wanted to marry her and take her to Wales. Her mother wouldn't hear of it. She was only eighteen. Then he had to leave for awhile; he said he'd return in six months. He died at sea and left Ruby with me. Of course, if he did exist, he might really have been just a drunken sailor."

"Conrad, let me tell ya. Ruby would never take up with a drunken sailor. She was proud. Proud. She wanted the best and made certain that she was seen only with the best."

"George, what did you mean when you said you weren't the favorite?"

I was sitting on the ottoman before him. Mary and Lorraine flanked us both. We were very close. George was wearing leather slippers, suit pants, and a sport shirt. We had brought him expensive cigars and he was holding one regally in his hand.

"Mustaffa liked Edmund best. He didn't care for anyone else, and never Ruby. She was a girl. He didn't care for women, I guess. Mom favored Ruby. That kinda left me out. Dad could never touch Ruby. If he ever laid a hand on her, Mom would have thrown him out. But he was always pushin' me. Always pushin'. I'd just grit my teeth and take it. Hoo. Once we were sittin' around the dinner table eatin'. I was thirteen years old — never forget it. Dad, for some reason, hit me with the back of his hand. Hit me *hard*. It knocked me right across the room. Jarred my teeth. Mom picked up a knife and told him that if he touched me again she'd kill him. I know he couldn't believe *that*. But that year I ran away."

"Where'd you go?"

"Oh, I went out West, you know. Bummed around. Montana. Texas. California. Roped horses. Was good at it."

"I heard you knew Tom Mix."

"Sure. Worked for him. Even was an extra in a picture out in Hollywood. Played a Mexican bandit. Can't . . . let's see . . . no, no, can't reee-member the name of that picture. I'll think of it sometime. Edmund could ride, too. When we was small we'd deliver horses to all these towns around here . . . ride all day. Newton, Somerville, Framingham. But at thirteen I up and lifted my feet. Funny thing about Dad. He left Mom, you know. But he couldn't give up Edmund. Edmund swore he'd kill him if he ever laid eyes on him again. But when Dad returned to see his favorite, they'd hug and take pictures. He never did visit anyone but Edmund, though."

I said, "So Ruby and Mom lived alone . . . until I came."

"That's right. You just came. No one explained you very

well. But they loved you. Everyone did."

"Another story I've heard is that Mabel (Edmund's first wife) asked Ruby to date a friend of hers on a blind date. Ruby was reluctant but Mabel insisted that he was a gentleman and it would be a great favor to Mabel if she would go out with him. So Ruby dated him and he raped her. Left her pregnant. But Ruby led me to believe that my dad was this Garth. What do you think?"

George rolled back to the base of his spine and puffed on his dying cigar. "I don't believe it. No. I don't believe it. Let me tell you why. Ruby was proud. She wouldn't go out with any blind date. And she hated Mabel. She would never do anything for Mabel. When Edmund married her, Mom was angry as hell. She thought that whole family was bad seed. And Mom and Ruby thought alike. Then Edmund divorced Mabel and married her sister. Mom couldn't believe it. Just couldn't believe it. So ya see, Mom and Ruby had no truck with them. I know Ruby wouldn't give Mabel the time of day."

Lorraine spoke now. "Ruby's mother, I guess she's George's too, for some reason liked me. I don't know why, but she liked me. Still, she told me very little. She cautioned me never to ask you any questions. She also said that in Jamaica they had maids and servants. They weren't poor as you have thought. They were high caste. When they came to America it was natural to associate with status. It couldn't be colored, so it had to be white."

George added, "You see, Conrad. If a girl came to the house and she was colored, Mom would steer her away from you. That wasn't the case for me. I came home with a colored girl . . . got her pregnant. Mom never said a word. And when I married Lorraine she approved. But with you it was different."

Lorraine was finding out about George for the first time. She was thankful we were finally talking. Mary was transfixed through all of it, and, as I later discovered, astounded by the control my grandmother had over all the family, and loving George and Lorraine more by the moment.

George went on, "Ruby was stuck with Mom. She couldn't get away; she was always beholden to Mom. When a man wanted to get serious with Ruby, Mom would call him in and tell him that Ruby was sickly and in weak condition. She frightened them all off."

"George, do you remember the time you and Mom came out to Camp Wadsworth to see me, when I was twelve? I was so ashamed that my friends would see your black faces that I never showed you around? You and Mom never said a word. You drove back to Boston and I felt ashamed. Remember that Sunday?"

George smiled. "No, I don't remember *that*."

"You don't remember that?"

"No. I don't."

"You don't *remember*?"

"I never saw you have a problem with things like that. No, that story surprises me about you."

We talked longer. When I tried to broach the subject of Edmund's underworld ties, George was evasive. When he railed at Ruby for her fantasizing and snobbishness, I fought back the tears. But it was good. Four, five times, George expressed how joyful he was that we wanted to share Thanksgiving with them. For the four of us, it was the warmest holiday we had ever experienced. All of us had been trapped in a family group controlled by an incredibly strong woman. George had been the closest to breaking out. On Thanksgiving Day, 1972, the two of us finally made it.

"We're gonna stay here a couple more years yet," George said. "Go down to Mississippi. Boston is bad. The house has been robbed twice. No sense when a woman has to fight off a robber in her bedroom. And steal cars — God, they steal cars. My car has had a burglar alarm that goes off if you tamper with the door, a toggle switch in the glove compartment that keeps the engine dead, and a brace that locks the steering wheel. No sense to that. We gotta little land. Gonna retire. Yeeees. Gotta little land and gonna retire."

I was free. Mary and I walked through the Public Gardens. On summer days there would be an art festival and white swans and rows of tulips and the world's smallest suspension bridge. The weather was crisp and good.

Before we left Boston, we had breakfast on the fifty-second floor of the Prudential Building. It looked out over all the commonwealth. Mary and I identified the Charles River and the Public Gardens and the old State House. Right below us, fifty-two stories down, was the Rice School. I was excited. "Look! There's the yard! Home plate was . . . right . . . there! You see? That green roof! Beansy Bhardo hit them out over that! There's left field where he snagged them! I played shortstop . . . right . . . there. . . . "

We looked at each other over tumblers of ice water and plates of toasted crumbs and bacon bits. I knew that the world had finally opened up to me. She knew. I'd never again fear this aging city . . . I'd ride humming wings into far-off places in a fascinating world, create paragraphs of words out of hushed events and fated peoples, and grasp happiness by its swan-soft neck until it screamed to please me more.

And as we held each other's eyes, she knew. That I was

her risk, her gamble. That it was no more "I." It was "we" . . . no matter what.

We were atop the city. I heard the roar of kids' voices echo from the narrow streets, bound up the steel canyon, then tail out to Boston Harbor, out to sea, never to be heard again.

Every bramble, branch, and bough . . . every
tapered tip, bared bark, and twig . . . point
upward to prick a thousand times the blue balloon
of sky. If any one bough would turn a knobby head
and peer into my pane and den, it would share
with neighbor bough a glimpse of immortality.
And they might murmur to each other, "He is first
man's duplicate. Tell the wind he, too, was
tempted. But he has brushed aside the fallen leaves
that scurried 'cross his path . . . the fallen leaves
of yesterday's old browns and golds and reds."